Millennials Guide to Work

How to Achieve Success and Respect

(The Young Professional's Guide to Getting Ahead at Work)

Robert Brown

Published By **Darby Connor**

Robert Brown

Millennials Guide to Work: How to Achieve Success and Respect (The Young Professional's Guide to Getting Ahead at Work)

ISBN   978-1-990373-76-3

No part of this guidebook shall be reproduced in any form without permission in writing from the publisher except in the case of brief quotations embodied in critical articles or reviews.

Legal & Disclaimer

The information contained in this book is not designed to replace or take the place of any form of medicine or professional medical advice. The information in this book has been provided for educational & entertainment purposes only.

The information contained in this book has been compiled from sources deemed reliable, and it is accurate to the best of the Author's knowledge; however, the Author cannot guarantee its accuracy and validity and cannot be held liable for any errors or omissions. Changes are periodically made to this book. You must consult your doctor or get professional medical advice before using any of the suggested remedies, techniques, or information in this book.

Table Of Contents

Chapter 1: What Do We KNOW ABOUT MILLENNIALS?

Why Is This Generation Called "Millennial" and "Gen Y"?

Where did the call "Millennial" originate? In 1991, generational historians Neil Howe and William Strauss tested American facts via a sequence of biographies that took a near have a look at the collections of tendencies that they detected in commonplace at some point of each technology agency related to twenty-one year time spans. At the time that they commenced out their paintings, generational research were now not commonplace. Naming the Baby Boomers was clean, however the following era, Generation X, didn't get a "actual" call. However, Howe defined that they decided on "Millennial" for the subsequent technology due to the reality they may start graduating high college inside the 12 months 2000. The 365 days 2000 furnished guarantees of each threat and prosperity, and the generation getting into adulthood at the century mark have emerge as visible by using way of older generations as similarly unpredictable.Five

Use of the moniker "Generation Y" or "Gen Y" virtually accompanied use of "Generation X." Given the closeness in the associated start years within the literature, Millennial and Gen Y are used synonymously in this e-book.

The call Millennial stuck after a 2013 Time magazine article entitled "The Me Me Me Generation" included the cohort in crucial and dismissive phrases. Google Trends, an online search amount tracker, showed a spike in utilization of the time period Millennial to consult this era from that thing. Most contributors of Generation Y have positioned the moniker derogatory.6 Certainly, there appears to be a extraordinary deal of terrible connotation related to the term "Millennial" in the minds of many. One can without a doubt look for "Millennial" online and find headline after headline that paints this era in negative mild. In a few regards, those in this era face unfair prejudice certainly because of large and undeserved stereotypes related to the choice.

Snapshot of the Millennial Generation

The Millennials had been born roughly between 1981 and 1995, elderly 21 to 35 at the time of my take a look at. Here I discover an define of what shapes their views.

Technology can be considered a photo of identity for Millennials. Gen Y uses all sorts of net and mobile phone era lots more than the older generations, for such every day sports as staying in touch with pals and own family, attending college and art work meetings, purchasing, banking and making an investment, producing current paintings, gambling video video video games, and searching films and TV.

Seventy-four percent of Millennials said they felt that new technology makes life much less tough. Fifty-4 percentage said it makes humans inside the direction of circle of relatives and pals. Fifty- percent noticed new technology as a manner to use their time greater successfully.7

Connection to circle of relatives is vital to the Millennial revel in of nicely-being. Millennials' mother and father tended to be very engaged with their kids, even at the identical time as divorcing, and Generation Y maintains with this own family-focused recognition. While 59% of Millennials in a 2014 Gallup ballot were unmarried or in no way married, the identical survey indicates that they count on to marry and to have youngsters. Nearly half of of single, 34-three hundred and sixty five days-antique Millennials have kids. Nine percentage of Millennials are in home partnership living preparations, and 36% are in multi-person families of three or more.Eight

Perhaps a number of those family arrangements are with the resource of monetary necessity, however similarly they reflect the manner Millennials are rearranging societal patterns at huge. They are delaying marriage and cohabiting as strategies to keep away from divorce, which many skilled of their non-public households or witnessed in the families in their pals. Additionally, Millennials are much more likely than the older generations to create families with LGBT companions, and till very in recent times, a number of those arrangements have no longer fallen into any own family elegance typically included in polls.Nine

Many Millennials have immigrant dad and mom or are immigrants themselves, which has made the generation extra ethnically diverse and tolerant than older generations. For Gen Y, gender and race are seen as genuinely reflecting unique memories and an array of evaluations to be assimilated and revered, in choice to being associated with hiring or faculty enrollment quotas. In maximum times, they've got not needed to count on two times about schoolmates and work colleagues who talk particular languages and placed on superb clothing and check high-quality non secular and cultural practices as a keep in mind of each day public existence.

The Millennials have additionally been shaped with the resource of:

Man-made failures: Environmental impacts which incorporates the Exxon Valdez oil spill and the Chernobyl nuclear twist of destiny.

War: The begin of the Gulf War in 1990 and the USA navy involvement in the Middle East ever because of the fact that.

Violence: The erosion of the belief of the overall protection of the area with airline bombings along with Pan Am Flight 103 over

Lockerbie, Scotland, college shootings like Columbine and Virginia Tech, the Oklahoma City bombing, and the activities of 9/11.

Marriage equality: The first issuance of identical-sex marriage licenses in Massachusetts in 2004 and the legalization of equal-sex marriages during the land in 2015.

President Obama: Election of america' first African-American president in 2008.

Economic downturns: The actual-time and deeply private family impacts of the housing bubble bust and the Great Recession that commenced in 2007, and the continuing burden of immoderate pupil debt and under-employment.10

Looking Ahead with Millennials

In spite of the previous research, Millennials are well on their way along their decided on course and inside the device of finding out an appropriate modifications they will be making of their worldwide. What developments in society will they be facing going in advance?

TRENDS IN THE WORKPLACE

Technology. The place of business is in reality era pushed via the Millennials' arrival. The right now exchange of facts over certainly any distance has made it feasible for agencies to perform seamlessly irrespective of whether or not or now not or no longer the primary players are remote places or at home. Computer technological data and facts generation careers have grown exponentially as more and more groups are searching out for era answers to hold up with the destiny.Eleven

These generation tendencies have facilitated the upward thrust of the on-name for economic machine, wherein employees can provide services to employers on a case-by means of-case foundation, over terrific distances, and with out the need for formal hiring and on-boarding. Over one-0.33 of Millennials are independent employees, whether or not by means of manner of preference (who prefer the association to the traditional 9-five) or through want (taking gigs at the issue to make ends meet). Some 32% of Generation Y see themselves in bendy working preparations within the coming years.12 Self-employment alternatives with corporations which encompass Lyft and Airbnb offer greater income possibilities which can be inner an character's control.

Employment shifts. Looking on the workplace large, permanent, detail-time, and short hiring is on the rise in 2017, and wages are growing as nicely. Employers are putting prolonged emphasis on employee "gentle talents" like first rate mind-set, reliability, and capability to artwork on a collection.Thirteen

Seventy-five million Baby Boomers are retiring and sixty five million Gen X human beings will not be sufficient to take their vicinity. The Millennials is probably challenged to fill the remaining training, manage, and capabilities gap.14

Work options. Millennials are technology multitaskers who see themselves as running smarter, not being lazy, after they choose to draft communications whilst at the teach and craft the finer elements in their proposals inside the café down the road. They pick to paintings to stay as opposed to live to paintings, and combine modern and earnings endeavors into their social life. Often, those attitudes located them at odds with employers with conventional frameworks and expectancies. Additionally, Millennials will be inclined to pick out steady super feedback, and within the occasion that they don't feel valued and happy of their pastime preparations, they will community themselves proper into a few other mission.15

TRENDS IN CULTURE

Generation Y is presently adapting to and influencing a massive type of societal adjustments which may be taking shape over the subsequent couple of a long term.

Life inside the cloud. By 2020, there can be about 5 billion internet users on 80 billion devices international. This connectivity will encompass paintings, home, and surrounding environments, turning them right proper into a "seamless experience." Our way of life alternatives will stay inside the cloud and travel with us as we navigate the offline worldwide. "Smart" (related, customizable, sensing, and self-monitoring) offerings, solutions, and governance may be the ordinary manner of life.16

Sustainability. Innovators will come in the direction of growing automobiles with zero emissions or injuries, cities with 0 carbon footprints, and factories with minimum environmental impact. Whether this can turn out to be truth, increasingly studies suggest that Millennials want and will pay extra for merchandise that useful resource sustainability, made through agencies that tangibly help powerful environmental and social effect.17

Affordable living. Millennials watched up near and private due to the fact the actual property disintegrate led own family and pals and pals into foreclosure, and the revel in has colored their enthusiasm for home ownership. They do not revel in, because the older generations did, that proudly owning a home is always part of the direction to wealth accumulation, even though for the most element, they see themselves proudly proudly owning a home subsequently.18 For now, they live with mother and father or hire, sharing housing with circle of relatives or others and finding smaller quarters they are able to responsibly come up with the money for. In line with modest housing needs, many Millennials want to be close to pals, paintings, offerings, and amusement locations, and a few opt for walking and cycling over owning a automobile.19

The evolving definition of achievement. Along with their housing alternatives, Generation Y is making distinct statements that run contrary to the lengthy-held perspectives of Baby Boomers and Generation X. Many Millennials do not diploma their success with the resource of greenbacks earned. They do need a straightforward earnings, however many are who opt to earn an awful lot less at a few detail they like to do in place of earn greater at some problem they dislike, they find it greater important to accumulate private dreams and make a terrific difference of their community.20

Embracing range and equality. Generation Y modified into born inside the course of a time of progressed immigration and decreasing Caucasian begin fees. Thus, they span a demographic hole among older, "whiter" generations and the racial and ethnic variety of coming Gen Z and extra youthful generations. They make up 23% of the entire U.S. Population; 27% of the whole minority populace are Gen Y. Millennials incorporate 30% of the balloting age populace, and 38% of the entire balloting age of minority voters. Thirty-8 percent of the group of workers are Millennials, and Millennial minorities make up 40 three% of the whole jogging age populace.21

In the 18–34 Millennial age bracket, fifty 5.8% are Caucasian. Diversity is broadening as Asians, Hispanics, and those who discover asor greater races comprise nearly 30% of the Gen Y populace in the U.S., and African Americans account for about 14%. This generation's ardour for advocacy and tolerance can be key in essential the country to greater a success racial range regulations.22

Diversity for Gen Y is broader than race or ethnicity. Equality is a first-rate difficulty, whether or no longer it's racial, sexual, educational, non secular, monetary, or in any other case. Many of those problems are being addressed within the better courts, and the rulings are having significant implications at the network, manner of existence, business employer, or maybe at the personal degree. Millennials experience that many factors of our society are damaged, and their energetic participation in politics may be key to healing a bargain of what they see as disappointing.

Political have an impact on. In 2008, Barack Obama acquired Millennial residents—18- to 29-twelve months-olds—thru 34 factors. The electorate additionally grew to come to be out in immoderate numbers, comprising approximately 18% of the citizens.23 Preferring not to be categorized and related to a political celebration, almost 60% of Millennials claimed to be impartial, many identified with Bernie Sanders, an avowed impartial and Democrat, and with Donald Trump, an interloper business chief without a political experience and few ties to the GOP reputation quo. Having positioned many employer and political scandals, this generation cautious of presidency and huge institutions had an affinity for a candidate who they perceived as representing trade and as credible in terms of approaches they provided their actual selves.24 The effect of the Millennials as a vote casting populace, coupled with immoderate unemployment amongst Millennials in extremely good elements of the U.S. And slim margins of help for Hillary Clinton in a number of key population segments,25 led a number of analysts to point to the Millennials as a big contributor to the results of 2016 election cycle. The lengthy and quick of it's far that Gen Y has the numbers to create the change they need.

Chapter 2: Values

Values are thoughts or standards of conduct that one holds to be vital. Our values, commonly framed thru way of societal norms,26 form the manner we do not forget what's taking location inside the international, the phrases we use to express ourselves, and the techniques we act in a single in each of a kind conditions. When we make choices, we are encouraged in a unmarried direction or some other via our values.

What Does Gen Y Value?

Professional and private values shape our priorities and the way we get up them in our personal lives and at artwork. In this financial ruin, we check what Gen Y values. As this generational cohort has end up the largest inside the workforce and begins offevolved offevolved to cope with an increasing number of manage positions, their values can have a greater and further impact at the workplace and in the long run on society as a whole.

Two crucial subjects tested in my take a look at had been personal and expert values. In order to recognize what motivates human beings, it's far beneficial to understand what they want out of life and the art work- or profession-related interests towards which they will direct their power.

Overview of Gen Y Personal Values

Starting with private values, the survey individuals have been requested What is most important to you for your existence right now from a private mindset?

For Gen Y, relationships become ranked first due to the truth the maximum crucial to the respondents as a hard and fast, determined thru manner of happiness, health, economic safety, profession, and faith.

In my have a study, Gen Y ranks each happiness and religion appreciably higher than do any of the alternative three cohorts. Not pretty, given the stark realities of the financial downturn of the beyond decade, economic protection is equally essential for all the era organizations.

One depend of a few hobby is the fairly excessive ranking of fitness, even over economic safety and career. Millennials, in assessment to older generations, view fitness and health as many small moves taken as part of their each day bodily activities in vicinity of a compartmentalized segment collectively with traditional medical practices. They consider the alternative generations at the primary priorities for fitness and health, like getting enough sleep, exercise, and water, however an lousy lot much less than half of of Millennials are possibly to plot beforehand with frequently scheduled checkups, vaccinations, preventive screenings, or obtaining scientific health insurance. Instead, they'll be greater willing to pursue possibility scientific practices together with natural, herbal, and non-toxic meals property, relaxation and unplugging from era, and keeping wholesome relationships.27

When the Millennials rank their personal values, each males and females agree that relationships and happiness are most vital. Gen Y Men and girls rank relationships most most of the options provided.

Overview of Gen Y Professional Values

Regarding professional values, I requested What is essential to you professionally right now?

The Gen Y respondents ranked the subsequent six value requirements so as of significance: making extra money, doing well in modern feature, work/life stability, selling, converting profession, and retirement.

Gen Y entered the personnel about 18 years within the beyond and masses of can be on their zero.33 or fourth process. Their values and expectancies have been influencing the place of work for almosta few years. The people in my have a observe had interest tenures that ranged from over 10 years with the identical agency (19%), six to ten years (20%), three to 5 years (19%), one to two years (25%), and much less than three hundred and sixty 5 days (17%).

Gen Y individuals famend the significance of monetary safety and rate the pride of a way properly accomplished, however they may be unwilling to sacrifice a personal lifestyles on the altar of career achievement. The finding that Millennials pick making extra cash is supported via way of using giant studies within the Deloitte Millennial Survey, which states that pay and advantages are the most vital finding out factors for Millennials selecting an business agency. In addition, many are going via existence degree adjustments related to beginning households and the associated monetary desires. However, with reimbursement being taken out of the picture, the subsequent maximum crucial identifying detail is capability to create and maintain a piece/existence balance.28

The Millennial emphasis on personal relationships and happiness highlighted inside the communicate on personal values need to in reality replicate a prioritization of social values over cloth advantage. It might be that experiencing and searching at economic hardships at the equal time as developing up cemented a deep want in Gen Y to never be placed into economic straits another time, while on the equal time driving home the fact that money troubles can bring about top notch disruption of important relationships.

Along the ones lines, the famous press notes that Millennials spend money on private relationships within the place of job lots more than do Gen X and the Baby Boomers.29 Other opinions on Gen Y display greater paintings pleasure once they sense they have emotional guide and friendship via their walking hours.30

In assessment to well-known opinion approximately Millennials and their cash conduct related to spending and saving, Generation Y sincerely places away a extra percentage of their paychecks than unique generations.31 They are pretty careful about how they spend, and do what they could to lessen fees the usage of such strategies as getting roommates, delaying home purchases, tracking spending with clever telephone apps, and budgeting smaller portions for sports than distinct generations are used to budgeting. Lower-paying jobs and financial hardships all through formative years have made those behavior a need. Saving for retirement is a sizable priority for Gen Y, as compared to one among a kind organizations of American earners.32

It is crucial to word some gender nuances. As inside the rating of personal values, men and women shared comparable professional values, best reversing the order of the top . Men ranked making extra money first and girls ranked doing well in the modern role first. When considering improvement planning, Millennial supervisors must hold in mind that this period wants to carry out nicely in their modern-day feature and that they expect to be compensated and financially rewarded for their overall performance.

Gen Y and the American Dream

In Generation Z within the Workplace, I first explored values within the context of 1's expectancies via generation agency based totally on efforts made and potential rewards acquired. This concept is important to the values dialogue for U.S. Citizens and is often associated with the concept of the American Dream. This high-quality have become famously described by means of James Truslow Adams in 1931, who stated that "existence ought to be higher and richer and fuller for every person, with opportunity for each steady with ability or success," not impeded thru the use of social rank, instances of begin, or different similar limitations.33 The American Dream as a first-rate is notably stated on in the famous press and modified into a key subject matter amongst candidates in the closing U.S. Election. I hold my exploration of this idea for Gen Y to offer angle on their expectancies.

Pursuit of training and home possession have normally been visible because the benchmarks of the American Dream, on the equal time as brilliant generations and exquisite monetary trends have squeezed extraordinary facets into or out of the wider know-how of the concept over time. As a rustic huge ethos, it implies the virtues and rewards of difficult artwork and backbone.

Many Americans have expressed situation that the traditional American Dream may moreover no longer be consultant of what the common American can without a doubt obtain. By and large, they element to the economic fact that many families have problem simply paying the payments on a monthly foundation, and don't have any possibility of saving for better training or shopping for a house. Other people have sought to modify their concept of the American Dream to encompass private achievement and attainment in their very very own set of beliefs.

To higher apprehend Gen Y's perceptions of the American Dream, I requested the test participants to rank six mind based totally on how critical they'll be to their version of the American Dream. They ranked the ideas on this order: being able to collect goals, economic safety, capability to pursue schooling, freedom of speech, home ownership, and building a legacy.

When the individuals of Gen Y were requested within the occasion that they believe that their version of the American Dream is workable, an awesome 88% stated YES! This reaction is decrease than Gen Z (90 five%) however nonetheless higher than Gen X (83%) or Baby Boomers (eighty%). I remember this excessive percentage encouraging, given the dramatic events that have customary their lives thus far. Overall, 87% of Americans in my take a look at although agree with the American Dream is possible.

Gen Y male and female respondents, at the same time as tested separately, expressed definitely particular priorities for his or her imaginative and prescient of the factors of the American Dream. Being capable of benefit goals and economic protection have been on the pinnacle for every, in spite of the reality that men valued fulfillment of goals over financial security, and the women vice versa. Home possession and building a legacy ranked at the lowest of the listing, which is not sudden, having already said that Millennials are delaying home possession in preference of lower expenses and better monetary financial financial savings.

As demonstrated inside the desk above, person men decided in this order: being capable of acquire dreams, financial protection, freedom of speech, capability to pursue training, constructing a legacy, domestic ownership. The women selected this order: economic protection, being able to attain goals, potential to pursue an schooling, freedom of speech, home possession, building a legacy.

Twelve percentage of the Gen Y members indicated that they felt the American Dream was no longer viable. I requested them to percentage a motive. Financial motives were the number one elements that seemed to restriction get right of entry to to the American Dream for this generational cohort. For eighty 4%, lack of cash have turn out to be the number one reason they felt the American Dream modified into not real for them. Debt, low wages, and typically dismal financial realities had been stated as other factors that made the American Dream appear unavailable.

While rate variety are a challenge for a few, at the entire, maximum Millennials are optimistic and firmly aware of the truth that their economic fulfillment is as tons as them. In reaction to the economic difficulties professional developing up, they workout, what some may also moreover additionally go through in thoughts, frugality as an regular dependancy. Even as such, they fee private connections and happiness more than the almighty dollar, preferring success on their very own terms over the extra predictable paths found with the resource in their elders.

It need to be stated that a current survey of the general population determined that kind of 1/2 of Millennials expect that the American dream is "useless."34 The difference among my survey and the overall population survey is that my respondents are all employed, at the identical time as fashionable populace surveys encompass entire-time employment, detail-time employment, underneath- or unemployment, and non-employment. This distinction offers essential context—my e book is aimed at the strolling population and reflects the ones perspectives.

Additionally, in different latest population surveys, amongst Millennials who had a college degree, nearly 60% agreed that the American Dream changed into achievable.35 Thirty-one percent of my survey respondents had some quantity of university education together with an Associate's degree; fifty two% had a completed a Bachelor's diploma or better.

This higher percent of college-knowledgeable respondents may account for the a whole lot higher than commonplace percent of good sized population Millennials who endure in mind the American Dream is doable.

Implications for Work Success and Career Paths

Job satisfaction, compensation, and splendid trendy overall performance typically come right down to how expectations and hopes healthy up with everyday realities: whether or now not you may accomplish what's required on some aspect near sufficient in your private terms which you don't enjoy a splendid deal of frustration. When on foot across generations, every so often the smallest versions in wondering and priority degrees can reason the maximum important misunderstandings and conflicts. Gen Y values boil all the way down to the truth that they need to have a earnings that allows them to satisfy their modern-day-day and destiny desires without too much disruption of their capability to gain fulfillment of their personal lives. Furthermore, they also want to do properly on the hobby and to beautify in their profession. Open exploration of those priorities can prevent a excellent deal of hysteria in administrative center discussions.

Consider the following statements:

"All my existence, I've typically achieved well and bought effective remarks approximately all my efforts, even if subjects didn't turn out exceptional. I were given reward for my efforts. In the beyond three months, I've taken on more obligations or perhaps inconvenienced myself. Why doesn't my boss take my request for a improve or vending seriously?"
– Gen Y Female

"When I commenced out out my profession, I had to in reality pay my dues with prolonged hours, taking up "growth" assignments and appearing the "unique duties assigned" more than I can rely. I've especially had on-assessment cycle promotions. She is a exceptional employee with masses of promise however I just don't get how someone thinks that taking on a few extra assignments for a few weeks technique they now deserve a beautify and selling. I'm giving her more to assist spherical out her competencies for the modern-day manner and set her up for destiny roles. Perhaps, I have to pick a person else…" – Gen X Female

It's clean that every of these human beings accept as true with that marketing have to be based totally totally on benefit, however each have super reviews approximately what advantage in fact is. In this situation, it'd be useful if they might have a candid conversation approximately their character reviews and expectations, and what the trouble seems like to every person worried. Open-minded and sincere communication is commonly the amazing way to return back to an records and forge agreements about priorities and development.

Practical Suggestions for Millennial/Gen Y Employees

No take into account what vicinity you decide in, competition for property, customers, and abilities is tough. Many employers are struggling to adopt and adapt to the methods that Gen Y values and expectancies are converting the place of business. Managers are balancing the desires of the organization in the direction of the want to pressure standard overall performance on the identical time as keeping their teams intact. Your wishes may be competing with many organizational priorities.

Stay real to your values, however make certain you and your supervisor are aligned. You fee your company, need to paintings hard and have time for the topics that rely most to you outside of your venture. It is critical that you ensure which you and your boss are on the identical net net web page about your paintings fashion, conduct, and need for your very very own time.

Be affected man or woman. It may be frustrating to sense that you typically must provide an reason of or justify your self—specially even as you believe the answers are clear out of your element of view. Perhaps your manager has one-of-a-kind values than you have were given. Find independent methods to explicit your non-public mind-set so others recognize wherein you're coming from. Instead of turning into shielding, reply with statements that display the advantages of your mind in terms of what your manager or co-personnel rate.

Make positive you and your supervisor are aligned on what difficult phrase seems like. While you may be committed to running difficult and are organized to area yourself into the exquisite position for receiving will increase and promotions, your manager or your supervisor's boss may additionally have a notable attitude. Your most essential values should manual your alternatives, but finding out what your supervisors anticipate is further critical.

Questions to Ask Your Supervisor

Preparing for Success

Practical Suggestions for Supervisors of Millennials/Gen Y

Your Millennial employee in all likelihood is fun the identical aspirations which you once had. Some are certainly starting their careers, others are mid-career, and all need to apprehend the way to position themselves for the subsequent step. Knowing whatnow, what must you tell your more youthful self about achievement and, greater importantly, how can you percentage this records to increase your employees?

Set them up for fulfillment. Perhaps at the same time as you commenced out your career, the expectancies for personnel have been superb than they may be these days. You would possibly have entered the place of work with an in-intensity training program or you will possibly had been left to problem-solve for your very own. Surviving a tribulation thru fireside experience isn't continually a badge of honor for Millennials. If they will be annoyed and can't see a path closer to sustained fulfillment, they will leave.

Encourage the realistic additives of profession improvement and placed the plan in area. Due to the monetary machine, many Millennials have had a not on time start to their careers and at the moment are eager to capture up. Think of tactics to beautify suitable art work behavior and abilities on the way to serve them well in any project, not absolutely for your branch. Millennials have severa years below their belt and function expectations approximately growing in their roles and careers.

Be apparent about repayment. Financial safety is vital to your Millennial worker, and so they may be centered on development and bonuses. It may be essential to have conversations approximately compensation in all bureaucracy (e.G., earnings, bonuses, holiday, special blessings) to control their expectations.

Recognize how they will be fashioned by using key non-public and expert values. From a non-public perspective, happiness and relationships ranked rather for Gen Y. Professionally, Gen Y values making extra cash and doing nicely of their current-day role. As you keep in mind the group environment and your manipulate style, don't forget how the great of your interactions and the paintings enjoy will be counted wide variety on your Millennial personnel. Coaching them to excel at the hobby and being clean about their opportunities to earn more money may be key to retention.

Chapter 3: Goals

What do Millennials need profession-wise once they look earlier with long-term desires in mind? Where do they enjoy they'll be in phrases of in which they in the end want to be of their careers, and what informs their options?

Four maximum essential factors have an effect at the lens via which Millennials view their dreams and possibilities: proudly proudly owning higher training, lower relative pay, student loan debt and un- or under-employment. These elements impact Millennial expectancies for their career interests.

Seeking to prepare themselves for a notable and countless future, Millennials went to college in droves. In addition, employers want a more informed and quite professional body of humans and, depending on the agency, are reluctant to lease all people without a degree of their location. However, Gen Y graduated to find out few jobs available, diploma or no longer. Many are not able to discover art work the least bit: eight% of 18- to 29-three hundred and sixty five days-olds have been unemployed in 2016, in evaluation to 3.7% of the overall American populace. Many others were compelled to take low-paying and detail-time jobs for which they may be over-educated.36

Millennials who're lucky enough to have found complete-time paintings have coped with stagnant pay, receiving handiest a 6% enhance from 2007 to 2014, in evaluation to 15% for the senior generational cohorts in the course of the equal seven-3 hundred and sixty 5 days time frame.37

How Does Gen Y Feel approximately Their Career Opportunities?

As a part of my studies, I asked the Gen Y respondentsquestions and gave them the opportunity to give an reason in their solutions. The first query: How do you rate your cutting-edge-day career possibilities? The rating alternatives were incredible, correct, average, horrible, and awful.

The majority of the respondents had favorable perspectives of their profession options. Seventy percent of Gen Y fee their career opportunities as nicely or better than appropriate. For a breakdown, 27% of Gen Y charge their profession opportunities as first-rate and forty three% price their profession opportunities as right. On the entire, Millennial guys are extra constructive than are their lady opposite numbers about future career possibilities.

Even with the behind schedule begin, Gen Y is positive about career opportunities:

27% of Gen Y are searching forward to incredible opportunities

70% of the Gen Y members (80% of men and sixty two% of women) rated their career opportunities as actual or remarkable

28% of Gen Y adult men rated their profession possibilities as awesome

26% of Gen Y ladies concept their profession prospects have been outstanding

Twenty-8 percentage of Gen Y person adult males fee their career possibilities as exceptional and fifty one% fee their profession opportunities as correct. In the test, 80% of Gen Y guys rate their profession possibilities as real or better than genuine.

Twenty-six percent of Gen Y Females fee their profession opportunities as extraordinary and 36% charge their profession opportunities as real. Sixty-percent of Gen Y Females price their career opportunities as right or better than correct.

What Makes Career Options Excellent for Gen Y?

After receiving their solutions about profession prospects, I invited the respondents to present an purpose behind why they answered the way they did. The maximum common reason mentioned for an awesome career outlook modified into that they love their mission (25%). The next maximum well-known reaction turn out to be a statement related to everyday delight with their lifestyles (14%). Theseforms of response account for 1/2 of of the replies. The open-ended responses are listed beneath.

Love my manner

Just love everything about my challenge

I love my life

Things have in no way seemed higher

It's everything I want, can't ask for added

I actually have pretty a few profession picks

I genuinely have a amazing procedure

I really have a exceptional challenge with room for increase and I plan to complete college to open up even extra possibilities

I am a trainer and I love wherein I paintings

I am doing very well and making what I need

I have no court cases

Because I'm happy

Getting better

It's the super activity I may additionally want to ever ask for

Because my economic scenario is terrific

Everything is first-rate and so is my profession

Because I am having a excellent time

I am surely loving wherein my profession is taking me

Seeing many opportunities in advance (14%), receiving genuine pay (9%), and noting the results in their very very own interest and tough work (nine%) have been the following maximum common motives cited for an splendid career outlook. Two motives were given for an

lousy career outlook, the primary being shortage of open positions, the second being no increase within the selected organization.

Enjoying one's vocation in addition to lifestyles in preferred topics to Millennials. These responses are consistent with the notion that Millennials vicinity high fee on well-known lifestyles happiness and making enough cash for their functions. Doing properly of their current feature is an important factor of the paintings-lifestyles balance equation due to the fact these finding propose that fulfillment from and at art work is vital to Gen Y.

Twenty-3 percentage of respondents stated that their career outlook became common, and 7% indicated that their career outlook became awful or awful. The reasons stated above for lousy prospects mirror the reality that the financial gadget has not recovered completely for each person. Millennials stay best at the identical time as their conditions are perceived as first-rate, but monetary realities temper enthusiasm while there may be problem making ends meet.

Are Millennials on Track for Their Job Goals?

The subsequent query I requested the have a check members modified into Are you on your perfect hobby for this diploma on your lifestyles? The solutions to pick from had been genuinely now not, in all likelihood no longer, perhaps, possibly sure, and sincerely sure.

Twenty-5 percentage of Gen Y respondents say they're virtually in their great manner and 36% of Gen Y say they may be possibly in their best approach. Sixty-one percentage of Gen Y say they're simply or possibly of their nice pastime.

Roughly the same proportions who indicated truly certain and possibly positive (61%) as to whether or not or not they were inside the proper interest for the cutting-edge degree of their lives moreover decided on incredible and desirable for their career possibilities (70%). Viewed on the side of numbers within the profession outlook phase above, task pride is honestly correlated to profession outlook. It might seem that those Millennials who are capable of discover correct jobs typically have a tendency to like them very masses and study their careers as being at the right track.

The male and lady survey contributors replied with kind of comparable numbers regarding what they concept of their profession opportunities. Sixty-4 percent of fellows and fifty 8% of ladies idea they had been genuinely or probably of their best jobs; 22% of males and 28% of girls stated that they've been virtually in their best jobs.

The majority of Gen Y women and men tended to experience that they have been on course.

22% of Gen Y grownup guys say they'll be surely of their perfect hobby and 40 % of Gen Y grownup men say they'll be in all likelihood of their nice interest

28% of Gen Y women say they may be clearly in their perfect way and 30% of Gen Y women say they're possibly in their high-quality interest

sixty 4% of Gen Y person men say they may be in fact or probably in their first-rate method

fifty eight% of Gen Y girls say they'll be truly or probable in their ideal undertaking

I invited the 8% of respondents who said they were honestly now not in their best challenge to offer a reason why. The responses are quite telling. Listed in order of the manner frequently they were given, the reasons are as follows:

In wrong characteristic. General dissatisfaction with the current feature (one-zero.33 of those who knew they truely weren't in which they had to be)

Weren't the usage of their schooling. That they had been in paintings that did no longer require the degree they possessed (one-fourth of the folks that knew they actually weren't in which they had to be)

Low pay. They felt beneath compensated.

High stress. Their manner or artwork environments have been too disturbing.

Lack of development. No room for merchandising at current venture

Settling for what they technique they'll get. Nowhere else modified into hiring

Interestingly,high satisfactory answers showed up some of the honestly now not responses.

I want to very very own my very private commercial enterprise employer

Don't enjoy current art work, thinking about a today's career

These individuals are conscious that they may be in the end on top of things of their futures and are capable of cope with mission dissatisfaction in phrases of personal duty and walking to obtain some aspect higher. This mind-set allows the notion that Millennials tend to reject what doesn't artwork for them and do what they must do to get beforehand on their non-public phrases.

Implications for Work Success and Career Paths

Many members of Generation Y came out of immoderate school and college to find out a whole lot much less than they had been promised in phrases of get entry to to jobs and promising profession tracks. Yet, for the maximum detail, they private the determination to get out of any rut they will discover themselves in. If they've got decided a terrific jogging state of affairs, they want to stay, and masses of have the pragmatism to rethink their path inside the event that they don't see achievement where they will be.

Consider the subsequent statements:

"I overheard the department heads final month complaining that the agency place of job froze will increase and hiring and promotions for the following six months, after my manager said I end up in truth due for a decorate and attention for the crew lead. Everyone wonders why I've been so depressed nowadays. I want the money and I turned into in fact hoping for the crew lead perks. I used to like it proper here and I can rarely drag myself in in recent times. I feel stuck." – Gen Y Male

"You recognize, I sense like I need a sparkling infusion into my career, but I don't recognise what it's going to be. Maybe I want to move check any other business organisation." – Gen Y Female

"I can't trust my ears. One of my managers is involved that his organization isn't satisfied. Perhaps they'll be happier in the event that they were unemployed. I recognize things are tough, however we aren't making our numbers this location. They really want to suck it up." – Baby Boomer Male

"I truly took a control feature at a contemporary day corporation, pleasant to find out that the man or woman I'm replacing have become allow pass due to the fact she misplaced half her employees internal a three hundred and sixty 5 days. Now I'm freaked out. How in the international can I be held responsible for individuals who certainly decide it's time to leave?" – Gen X Female

More and extra research is pointing to the idea that happiness at art work is not simply the byproduct of actual typical overall overall performance, suitable pay and perks, and improvement opportunities. Rather, pride with artwork and giant bonds with art work colleagues are getting critical factors in a success engagement with procedure and profession. An examination of an extensive series of research permits the notion that a immoderate diploma of private happiness is associated with first-rate influences in many areas of lifestyles, along with highbrow and bodily health, relationships, earnings, and social or community involvement.38

For the Millennial employee who can articulate her actual goals for the administrative center, and for the Millennial supervisor who is privy to that his personnel in reality do have motives aside from capriciousness for leaving their jobs, beneficial conversations may be started out out round what's crucial in phrases of what it takes to live and invest within the commercial enterprise employer. Situations that look one way to at the least one celebration also can appearance without a doubt one-of-a-type to one in all a kind occasions.

Millennials are realists who realize the way to cope with a whole lot a whole lot much less than perfect situations in the event that they have some degree of manage. They disconnect. They go away. And, they post their reports on social channels for the complete worldwide to appearance (and decide your employer). Supervisor transparency can pass an extended manner towards aligning Millennial humans' expectations, and gaining their help and cooperation.

Even if things are remarkable, there may be tactics to make matters higher. If business corporation is unsure, silence from control could have an unwelcomed effect on employees. Bringing all people to the desk to problem-treatment or provide pointers can help control expectations and make paintings environments greater inclusive. New mind can revolutionize departments and organizations while employees and supervisors alike are invited to be open and speak what they would really like to peer take location. And if answers are not proper now available, being honest approximately the state of affairs also can be useful, as to keep away from personnel wondering that you are hiding the fact from them.

Practical Suggestions for Millennial/Gen Y Employees

Careers are marathons, no longer sprints. They require training, difficult paintings, and investment in your aspect. You will want to be affected man or woman occasionally due to the fact the wishes of the organisation and the possibilities for development and revenue will increase might not commonly line up along with your expectations. However, you can set your self up nicely.

Focus on doing the incredible manner you can to your cutting-edge-day function. Your career plan may be focused on having quick stents in a role. Once you experience you have got were given mastered it, you're prepared and assume to transport up into the following project. Some organizations do have fast-transferring career tracks and faucet or circulate know-how outside of scheduled overall performance cycles. However, most organizations have annual or biannual time frames while promotions or increases may be considered. The secret's to perform properly in your function and probably even over-perform so you are a better candidate while the opportunity arises. Doing so can even set you up for achievement on your next feature.

Broaden your ability set. Explore tactics you may add charge via searching out to gain new abilties and art work reviews. Consider making use of for jobs on the identical become aware of or grade level to research a latest ability set or enterprise, if transferring up isn't an opportunity. Identify lessons you could take to increase your expertise and sharpen your potential units to make your self more valuable on your employers and institution.

Get geared up for control. Perhaps you're years some distance from dealing with human beings. Maybe it's your subsequent step. Or, being a manager won't additionally be to your profession radar show show. In any case, the reality is that as Baby Boomers maintain to depart the group of workers, greater possibilities turns into to be had. Consider getting organized your self now. Are there any stressful conditions or opportunities at your contemporary workplace that you can address to illustrate greater of your abilties in your boss? Or, do you have got got had been given a great concept that you'd need to have the group attempt to put in force? Volunteer to persuade a bypass-feature crew or project to get exercising and display yourself.

Consider advancing in your function somewhere else. Sometimes personal pastimes aren't aligned with available opportunities at your commercial enterprise business corporation. If you've talked alongside aspect your supervisor and the alternate you need isn't always to be had inner a time body that suits your expectations, you can want to make a trade. If you could, take a look at out other departments or corporations that may have more room for improvement and the compensation you want.

Setting Priorities

In this situation, if all matters had been identical, moving to the stylish interest looks like an clean preference with a score of "eleven." However, on the equal time as elements which incorporates tour, advantages, and venture come into play, the selection to live for your present day-day function with a multiplier rating of "28" may also furthermore win out and lead you to engage in a chunk extra idea about what truly matters at this component.

Practical Suggestions for Supervisors of Millennials/Gen Y

Many of your Millennial personnel are finding themselves in a terrific area, on the equal time as others may be suffering or considering some element else. Make a determination to help your personnel find out pleasure in phrases of normal average overall performance and reference to others.

Offer constructive remarks when it is warranted. Generation Y is used to instantaneous comments for his or her thoughts because of their commonplace use of social media within the direction in their young adults. Give them what they need to honestly perform what you're asking of them, along side encouraging words. Be considerate about requests for better or particular paintings, and make certain you furthermore may additionally proportion sincere assurances concerning what you admire approximately their paintings.

Be easy approximately their alternatives. Be positive to permit them to understand they're valued in their modern characteristic and be inclined to be open and sensible about their profession prospects. Whether you're providing hobby alternatives within your business enterprise or laterally inside your enterprise, inspire your personnel to find out and do what they may be capable of to position themselves for moving on inside the event that they've mastered their contemporary characteristic. Coach them to transport sideways even as you may, and be supportive of their alternatives to transport on inside the occasion that they do.

Chapter 4: Work Environment Preferences

As groups trying to find methods to get the maximum out in their frame of workers and assemble leaders, there was top notch interest paid to the largest technology within the place of business—Millennials. Recent articles have loads to mention approximately massive developments within the American workplace, several mainly that include the Millennial technology in particular strategies. Information access and generation is remodeling the place of work, and Millennials are within the thick of it. Millennials are also the maximum knowledgeable generation thus far, bringing information and know-how to undergo early of their profession tenures. They are starting conversations about cultural variety in the administrative center. At the equal time, Gen Y has a awesome attitude in phrases of compensation and pay.

Members of Gen Y in the employees are somewhere between 21 and 36, absolutely getting started out or a pair jobs into their career. What form of administrative center do they need to thrive in each day? What are they seeking out? Let's take a look at the contemporary-day American place of business and the Millennial options which may be shaping it, in terms of their idea of a terrific interest, and in terms of a fantastic manager.

Recent Trends within the American Workplace

Information and Technology

No you could deny that technology has created mind-blowing exchange within the art work environment, which includes how, on the identical time as, and in which we art work. Remote artwork preparations were facilitated through the on the spot alternate and accessibility of statistics in its many paperwork, from documents to audio/video to live feed interactions in the course of the globe. According to the U.S. Bureau of Labor Statistics, in 2015, approximately 24% of employees did some or all in their work from home.39 Flex-time, progressive paintings spaces, and outsourcing also are converting each day paintings, and there are greater belongings available in phrases of in-house services to enhance the health and productivity of employees.forty

Millennials, coming of age as technology brought those changes to the manner of exertions, strongly pick out person-quality interfacing with the software and apps they use on a every day basis. Some reports display that they pick to resolve their personal issues and skip far from apps and web sites in which they may be capable of't effects solve troubles regarding function or purchase, locating their answers in the big repository of various alternatives available. This tendency has pushed demand for exceptional patron enjoy in tech development.41

Even in the event that they have got to discover, produce, or tweak it themselves, Millennials anticipate to use specialised software application which incorporates industry-specific accounting or stock or consumer manage structures, or training software application, that can interface sooner or later of critical structures inside the place of business, a protracted manner beyond the use of Microsoft Word and Excel. The proactive supervisor can take advantage of enter concerning era from their Millennial employees, who is probably adept at developing with every small method tweaks similarly to custom upgrades to strength organization productiveness.forty

Pay

Considering that Millennials are 50% more likely to be university educated than earlier generations and they're the large driving pressure in the back of a 70% growth in place of business productivity,40 3 there may be some accurate judgment that would purpose the perception that Gen Y can be the quality paid generation up to now. However, many research are finding that this is not the case.

Examining statistics from the U.S. Census Bureau's Current Population Survey, one researcher checked out the yearly income for a Millennial in 2014, a Gen X member in 2004, and a Baby Boomer in 1984, every earner at the age of 30. With the numbers adjusted for inflation, nowadays's 30-365 days-olds are bringing in as thousands as a 30-twelve months-old in 1984, this is, $19.30 steady with hour. Ten years inside the past, 2004's 30-three hundred and sixty five days-vintage earned a greenback more regular with hour than in recent times's employee.40 4 The Young Invincibles agency examined Federal Reserve records for 25- to

34-year-olds in 1989 (now greater youthful Baby Boomers) and for 25- to 34-one year-olds in 2013 (now Millennials), installing that these days's Millennials are making about 20% a lot less than their dad and mom did, and characteristic a decrease net actually nicely worth, on the identical time as being extra informed.45

It is an easy truth that, for any range of reasons, the ones coming of age at some stage inside the financial disaster of 2008 located themselves taking jobs at depressed wages, which has persisted to avoid their ability to benefit the equal dwelling necessities as the sooner generational cohorts.

This said, other critiques discover that Millennials are inclined to take less pay and different benefits (which include retirement, scientific clinical medical insurance, paid time without work, and possession of part of the enterprise corporation) in trade for higher artwork/lifestyles stability, which incorporates career development, significant work, and a high-quality employer life-style. Six in 10 Gen Y people may additionally want to surrender $7,600 on common in exchange for extra incredible "remarkable of hard work life."forty six Compensation is vital, but there can be more flexibility in housing, transportation, and intake alternatives than there may be at paintings. Once a mission provide is normal, precise capacity options are removed, together with different viable companies to research from and contribute to, a excellent employer of co-employees, and a unique favored place of work manner of life.

Diversity

At the identical time that era is changing the day-to-day face of the place of business, there is moreover improved variety in age and ancient past of coworkers. Millennials are greater comfortable talking approximately range and inclusion at artwork than Gen X and the Boomers. In truth, forty seven% of Gen Y considers variety and inclusion to be important factors at the same time as thinking about a contemporary method, in evaluation to 33% of Gen X and 37% of Baby Boomers. While personnel of every age agree that employers setting an emphasis on variety and inclusion (D & I) makes their region of employment better, Millennials have a tendency to mention that such practices make the workplace a better location to art work and increase opportunities for all employees. Gen X and Baby Boomers are much more likely to mention that the boss is implementing "D & I" guidelines on the way to make the organization appearance better to outsiders and because of out of doors strain.47

According to the U.S. Census Bureau, forty four% percentage of Millennials become aware about as a minority race or ethnic organization other than non-Hispanic, single-race white.48 Eleven percentage of

Millennials are kids of immigrant dad and mom, accounting for the most vital quantity of 2d-generation Americans than any previous generational cohort.forty 9

Education

Americans believe that it takes every technical and social savvy to navigate the place of job effectively. Competence with computer structures and being able to work with human beings from extensively numerous backgrounds rank as maximum important, beforehand of education in writing, communication, math, and technological understanding.50

U.S. Employment tendencies aspect to increasing name for for superior schooling, training, and revel in for a far wider sort of industries, and a decline in need for bodily and manual skill. Education and healthcare are experiencing the first-class corporation boom, assisting to create this want for more education and education. Fifty-4 percent of people, representing all schooling degrees, agree that their destiny achievement at paintings will involve continuing expertise development, predominantly in similarly formal training.51

In 2010, Pew Research pronounced that half of of Millennials favored to go to university. Thirty- percent intended to visit graduate college or a expert college. Sixty-5 percent of people who had give up desired to go again. Of the 48% that did no longer hold in faculty, 36% stated they could not come up with the money for it, and 35% said they didn't have time—possibly because they were too busy walking. Only 14% stated they didn't need any extra schooling. One in 10 Millennials have been strolling whole-time and going to school.fifty

Seven years later, Generation Y is simply the amazing knowledgeable cohort thus far in America: one 0.33 of Millennials age 26–33 have carried out a Bachelor's degree or higher.fifty three Twenty-one percentage of men and 27% of girls age 18–33 had finished at least a Bachelor's degree.fifty four

As the economic system shifts to a statistics base instead of a tough paintings base, those who've no longer pursued education beyond immoderate university are having a miles greater hard time making ends meet. They face constantly decrease wages and higher unemployment expenses, tons greater so than did Generation X and Baby Boomers who had best excessive faculty education.fifty 5

In my have a look at, 1% had a whole lot less than a excessive school diploma, and sixteen% had ended their education with immoderate school. By evaluation, 28% had finished a Bachelor's diploma and 24% had lengthy past at once to do submit-graduate to place up-doctorate artwork.

Millennials and Work Preferences

Where are Millennials walking? Sixty-eight percentage of the survey respondents were employed at for-earnings corporations at survey time. Twelve percentage had been in instructional settings and each other 12% in non-profits. The 8% very last had been operating in authorities roles.

Given the chance to pick the choice that maximum carefully matched their task discover, one region of the agency stated management or director and eight% said vice chairman or senior vp, C level authorities, or president/CEO. There become one proprietor/entrepreneur the various respondents, and one intern. Seven percent were instructors or professors. The different possible lessons blanketed assistant, analyst, companion, representative, professional, coordinator, and special.

Corresponding with modern-day employment trends, the maximum represented agency grow to be healthcare and medical-related at 15%. The subsequent maximum represented company changed into training in any respect tiers, for 13.Five%. Twelve percentage of respondents had been employed in retail. Construction and production accounted for 11% of the respondents, located with the aid of using statistics offerings and facts at 7%, finance and insurance at five%. Eighteen percent of the respondents were in agriculture, forestry, fishing, or looking; arts, enjoyment, or hobby; broadcasting; communications and public individuals of the circle of relatives; authorities and public manage; laptop and electronics production; hospitality; crook and advertising and advertising and marketing and advertising.

What type of hours are Millennials installing? Two percentage of respondents (all girl) stated they have been no longer walking (in between roles) on the time of the survey, and three% said they favored now not running.

Fewer than 6% of the Gen Y respondents worked a notable deal an awful lot much less than 20 hours in line with week, and seven% said that fewer than 20 hours each week is probably perfect. The majority of Millennials, 57%, are on foot 21–40 hours each week, and fifty nine% stated that they'll decide upon a 21- to 40-hour art work week. Thirty-five percentage are working forty one or extra hours in step with week, at the same time as best 31% need to be walking this thousands.

More girls than men stated strolling 21–40 hours in line with week, fifty 8% to fifty five%, and the identical possibilities for every have been walking forty one–50 hours—28%. Eight percentage of person adult men and six% of girls have been running 51 or more hours consistent with week.

Twelve percentage of guys indicated that they might discover a lot much less than 20 hours high-quality, along 3% of women. Fifty-four percentage of men in comparison to sixty 3% of girls determined 21–40 hours per week excellent, and 26% of men in evaluation to twenty-eight% of ladies idea that 41–50 hours in keeping with week can be quality. At the same time, more ladies than men, 4% to 3%, stated that they preferred now not to work.

Aside from the sweet spot of 21–forty hours every week, Gen Y is taking walks greater than they want to artwork. This corresponds with the Millennial desire for paintings/life balance, while having to paintings sufficient hours to pay their dues in phrases of career responsibilities and earning a dwelling to pay their payments.

Gen Y and Ideal Job Tenure

Eighteen percent of the respondents of a February 2016 survey with the aid of Jobvite indicated that they exchange jobs every one to a few years, and 16% percentage will change jobs in four to five years. Millennials are said to have the very first-rate serial worker charge: forty two% alternate jobs each one to a few years for the ones 18 to 29 years of age. Fifty-five percent of Millennial ladies mainly will exchange jobs each one to 3 years.fifty six

How do the Millennials in my take a look at examine? Thirty percent of the Millennial respondents have been at their modern-day-day role for three to five years, 34% of the guys and 26% of the women. Twenty-seven percentage famous have been with their contemporary company one to 2 years, 24% of the men and 28% of the girls. They plan to stick round more than the national not unusual stated above; but, 10% intend to live wherein they are for one to two years, and 23% intend to live wherein they may be for 3 to five years, for an entire of 33%. This breaks down into 37% for guys making plans to stay with their cutting-edge-day employers for one to five years and 29% of ladies making plans to stay in which they're for the same one- to 5-yr span.

Twenty-five percent of the examine individuals have been with their modern enterprise for 6 to ten years, 27% of adult men and 24% of ladies. This represents extra or lots less a quarter of Millennial employees who have stayed positioned 5 years longer than the countrywide common of challenge tenure.

What's the longest process tenure of Millennials inside the survey? Seven percentage of every males and females had already been with their contemporary organisation for 10 or more years. It is first-rate and provoking to study that 39% and 38% respectively intend to be with their modern-day organisation for 10 or extra years. These Millennials have decided a place to flourish professionally and in my view and are invested in a solid future in which they're.

At the identical time, 7% indicated intentions of leaving their cutting-edge enterprise business enterprise after an awful lot much less than a three hundred and sixty 5 days's tenure: 3% of person males and 14% of ladies. I asked a motive for leaving from folks who stated they would depart in advance than a year modified into up. The responses ran as follows:

Not happy with current assignment

I would really like a new task at a one-of-a-kind commercial enterprise employer

It's now not a wholesome environment

I am presently carrying out a search for new employment

Because I am going to artwork in my career after graduating

Need a exchange

Plan to get degree

Don't like my organisation corporation

Another hobby opportunity with extra room for advancement

I dislike my approach

The most not unusual reason given modified into dislike for the state of affairs, which lines up with the Millennials' precedence of a bit/life stability, being capable of like their work and their employment lifestyle.

Gen Y and the Boss

Most jobs in recent times require excessive levels of leadership and verbal exchange potential if you want to successfully coordinate teams and obligations. Flexibility and willingness to try new topics are essential. Supervisors are in key positions to educate their greater more youthful employees those crucial capabilities and draw on their more expert people to help create the only and amenable subculture feasible.57

As with any generation cohort, Millennials have very smooth thoughts approximately what constitutes a superb boss and what is unacceptable. Some of the maximum vital subjects supervisors can do are to be open and respect the shape of worker their Millennial worker is and spend time learning her or him as an person with a very particular individual and set of capabilities.

Gen Y values and unearths extraordinary benefit in interaction with out hierarchy and a unfastened exchange of information that results in negotiation and answers. In the administrative center, this interprets into first rate potential for comments, each great reinforcement and fantastic grievance, and the choice to speak about issues without pinnacle-down criticism and orders. As may additionally any diligent worker, Millennials want sufficient schooling that permits you to perform their obligations, and they want to be directed and challenged towards success as properly. Millennials see supervisors lots less as authority figures who want to be obeyed and handled with deference and extra as lead institution participants who help make the administrative center characteristic nicely. Coworkers are taking component equals to resource and be supported with the useful resource of manner of. Ultimately, happiness is determined in massive art work and emotional connection and pride that subjects in existence are going as well as viable.

In this book, I desired to attention on what Millennials want in a boss and the manner positive control practices can effect the Gen Y adventure at art work.

How Gen Y Feels about Their Boss

Study people had the possibility to fee their modern manager as a pacesetter the usage of first-rate, proper, common, poor, or lousy. Compared to the alternative generational cohorts inside the have a look at, Gen Z changed into the satisfactory cohort with a more percent (eighty four%) than Gen Y that indicated they perception that their boss grow to be an amazing or wonderful leader; fewer Gen X (70%) and Baby Boomers (sixty six%) gave an first rate or ideal rating.

Seventy-six percent of Gen Y human beings taken into consideration their boss an excellent or real chief; 37% of respondents rated their boss wonderful as a pacesetter, and 39% rated the boss as suitable as a pacesetter. The very last 24% decided on not unusual, terrible, or awful to explain their boss.

Along with their score, contributors were asked to offer an purpose at the back of their options. There have been many reasons given for an wonderful boss score. The solutions given the most needed to do with resource and care for individuals (most frequently mentioned), incredible manage competencies (subsequent maximum cited), data of the economic company, and proper communique. Other Gen Y respondents had the following to say:

Advocates for her employees, humorous and easygoing

Because she cares about every employee and his dignity

She is particularly beneficial, motivating and desires to see you be successful

Very records and sincere

Helps you on every occasion

Friendly

They are sincere and clean and really informed

She is privy to her process interior and out, is an first rate instructor, strives to make every body better and may take manage in chaotic situations

She took the time to pay attention and recognize me and help me expand.

Have a obvious communications method within the direction of all personnel, especially in sharing alternatives about whether someone should have a selling or no longer. Also, superb awesome in personality.

Several participants had no problem identifying what they disliked the most approximately their bosses.

The energy to sincerely now not care

He is a narcissist jerk

Out of contact owner manager with a huge mind-set

Hardly ever gift. Loquacious and unproductive.

Incompetent

There is not any assist or state of affairs for employees

In my take a look at, Gen Y respondents gave precise feedback as to what their supervisors need to do that they felt may want to assist them to reach their current function. Respondents had been given the opportunity to answer the ones two questions: 1) Please listing one detail you would like your manager to START doing to help you be greater a hit on your position; and a couple of) Please list one element you would really like your supervisor to STOP doing to help you be more a success for your role.

Only 6% said that there has been not anything they may ask their supervisor to start doing that could growth their possibilities of venture success, which suggests a widespread feel of consolation with the approach and fashion of their cutting-edge supervisor.

What Does Gen Y Want Their Bosses to Start Doing?

Gen Y respondents in my have a look at shared very particular feedback on how their managers can assist them be more a success of their roles. The maximum not unusual response had something to do with searching their supervisors to really lead, together with pleas to be bolder in disciplinary motion.

Try being extra of a leader in choice to in reality "going with the go with the flow"

Step as lots because the plate and now not allow exceptional employees step over her

Being there more often

Be present at the facility so they'll efficiently offer beneficial comments.

Taking rate and being greater assertive and vocal leader

Grow a spine with co-personnel who won't pull their very personal weight

Be a pacesetter and perhaps paintings

Disciplining coworkers

Grow a backbone

Fourteen percent particularly favored their bosses to assist them be successful wherein they had been and broaden through the usage of education them what they needed to understand, pointing them in the proper path, and simply training them.

Training

I would like him to assist me with matters I won't recognize tons approximately.

Offer schooling

Teach me new strategies

Teach me extra about being a mod

Give us more hints

Better guidance

I count on that my manager need to higher train the human beings which may be coming in as a current day worker.

Teach extra

Find tasks for me to do to bring together my resume.

Continue to provide me advice and guide me in the right path

Help me find out analyzing opportunities

Give us greater improvement possibilities and greater direction as to what training we ought to be doing to enhance our skills

Answer cellular phone calls, so I ought to get an answer on what's extraordinary to do

Giving me input on the manner to excel.

Training me in unique regions to see what my complete functionality is

Help us thru displaying us better techniques to get our work performed faster and extra green.

Provide me with better equipment to exceed. Demonstrate task for my boom in the feature.

Ten percentage preferred greater direct remarks as to strengths and weaknesses, correction, and advantageous grievance. Some asked to certainly be saved inside the loop extra. Some preferred their bosses to listen greater.

These responses confirm for us that Millennials do indeed strongly choice bosses they may be able to respect, leaders who will in truth lead, and offer situations and feedback with a purpose to assist them to be successful.

Six percentage of the respondents indicated that they desired more responsibilities and control opportunities. Six percentage each preferred higher pay or merchandising. Another 6% wanted the supervisor to regulate hours assigned simply so paintings may be achieved, workloads lessened, dependability validated, and schedules be dispensed fairly. Another 6% requested for higher conversation, clearer dreams, and better delegation.

Other repeated comments protected requests to prevent micromanaging and consider that subjects had been getting executed right, and that the boss respect particular manage styles. Listen to me, be nicer, and care approximately employees modified into requested, as have been organisation, teamwork, and assist from the boss. Four respondents requested acknowledgement and appreciation. Two favored transparency and honesty from their bosses.

Two respondents stated that they desired help with education troubles, such as extra time to get a diploma and help with training payments. Two desired their superiors to assist them with personal economic savings plans and making an funding in the employer. Finally, reflective of the Millennial preference for specific work-lifestyle conditions, numerous supplied some of techniques that topics may be made higher, along side:

Make subjects more a laugh

Make it sincere for both man and woman employees to speak together

Assure equality between personnel

One element I would like my manager to begin doing is ask extra questions as to how we are able to enhance our art work region

The "place of work lifestyle" subjects to Millennials, and it includes topics that distinct generations might likely don't forget private issues for which the administrative center isn't responsible. However, the supervisor who can do even a little bit inside the course of understanding and facilitating the ones place of business alternatives may additionally have a much better chance of keeping employees who need to art work difficult and be successful in which they will be now.

What Does Gen Y Want Their Bosses to Stop Doing?

A sudden 24% of Millennials couldn't listing something they desired their boss to forestall doing in order for them to be greater successful, irrespective of the truth that the rest had a large preference of responses. For the maximum difficulty, they expressed choice for the equal matters in the ones answers that they did in the answers to the query approximately what the boss may want to start doing, in reality the usage of honestly one in all a kind phrases. Along the strains of individuals who preferred their bosses to develop a backbone and deal with enterprise, 4 humans preferred their manager to forestall being any such coward and pushover. Similarly, eight% favored their supervisor to stop being absent, forestall being lazy, and forestall being unengaged.

Six percentage preferred their boss to forestall micromanaging them, and another

6% wanted their boss to prevent nagging and putting needs on them. Three individuals desired their bosses to stop making assignments outdoor their roles.

There have been many requests to forestall disrespectful conduct along with evident, speakme down, shutting down employee ideas, being essential, being judgmental, and being sarcastic. Favoritism, gossiping, yelling, rudeness, ignoring issues, terrible thoughts-set, and unprofessional or immature behavior had been exceptional topics employees favored stopped. Two wished their supervisors to save you looking for to save you their vending;preferred their managers to stop status inside the manner of progress:

Discouraging me from pursuing a specific road due to the fact he thinks I'm inadequate and received't attain fulfillment.

Not letting me go together with better administrative center

Doing things the vintage fashion way and include the extremely-modern-day methods of the usage of era

Preventing development/trade

Other responses consist of:

Stop reassignment of my subordinates.

Stop chatting a lot with the personnel approximately personal rather than professional time table.

Stop passing off ridiculous obligations that don't have any considerable impact on our corporation.

Maybe forestall having to check the whole lot.

Stop ordering us spherical and turn out to be a frontrunner

One issue I would really like my manager to save you doing is being too cussed.

Complaining to anyone that nobody respects her

He wants to prevent tripping

He is excessively chatty. So I would really like a whole lot less of that so I can be extra efficient.

Stop blaming unique humans for things he become speculated to do and forgot to do.

Patronizing

Hinting at destiny changes with out element or any idea even as matters will exchange or perhaps if they'll alternate. It genuinely creates uncertainty and employees worry approximately topics that might never show up.

Stop being dumb

Being inside the place of business for a long term length, busy sure. But go out now and again and make conversations.

Making a massive deal of small, quite uncommon oversights

As stated earlier than, the place of job surroundings may be very important to Millennials, not just the art work they're doing. A unique boss can go an prolonged manner in the direction of developing worker delight without a doubt via being a nice, engaged, and proactive leader.

A excessive percentage of satisfaction with the boss and immoderate expressed cause to stay with present day-day employers suggests strongly that many Millennials have located their region to stay, contribute, and increase. This must be encouraging to supervisors who probably dread hiring Millennials with the concept that they will be no longer possible to please and is probably quitting as fast as they're on-boarded. Understanding what your Gen Y employees really want and accommodating them as a good buy as feasible will purpose them to glad and efficient people of your crew.

Implications for Work Success and Career Paths

The historic economic information of the 2000s recession explains Millennial issue with finding proper jobs, handling college, and making-ends-meet debt, and casting off marriage, own family, and domestic looking for. Thus, the coins and improvement are important. Adeptness with generation and the efficiency that it offers makes them query the want to set up paintings the manner it's normally been, whether or not or not or no longer in cubicles or at great hours. It is plain that Millennials have a selected set of priorities that define some of the parameters in their careers.

Gen Y is ready to devote for the lengthy haul. They want to make the area a better location, at least their a part of it. They need to art work with a mentor or coach instead of a advanced. Or they'd choose to artwork for themselves. They select out collaboration to competition. They want freedom to work even as and the manner it makes feel to them, in choice to the manner of existence properly-set up administrative center practices.58

My check suggests that if the artwork, the repayment, their boss, or the social surroundings at paintings are not proper, Millennials have no problem transferring at once to a higher state of affairs.

Consider the subsequent statements:

"The interview have become quite perfect the alternative day, however after I requested about performance critiques and selling schedules, they definitely glanced at every exquisite, gave some lame nonsensical answer and moved at once to the subsequent question. So there's each other area I can plan on simply swimming along side out steerage till I get so irritated I stop. How are you capable of run a corporation without your human beings understanding what it takes to be successful?" – Gen Y Female

"I can rarely hold my cool on occasion. Why are the ones kids usually chatting over the cubicle partitions about topics that have nothing to do with art work? Some soccer meetup they've taking area, her teen, his dad's most cancers... If they need to be pals, they want to do it after artwork. I have a branch to run right right right here." – Baby Boomer Male

"So I counseled our HR manager how I noticed on Facebook how the contemporary-day hurricane left certainly one of our coworkers homeless and endorsed that we can also need to perhaps crowdsource to elevate cash to assist them out. He truly stared at me for a bit, then said a few aspect approximately now not being in reality high quality that became appropriate. So an lousy lot for our organisation values of worrying about people. It subjects, doesn't it?" – Gen Y Male

"I'm dropping my employees left and proper and I don't recognize why. They come, artwork hard, live for 3 or so years, then they're long long gone. I've bent over backward to get them better blessings, finished a few remodeling throughout the vicinity, permit them to set their schedules, but not some component appears to manual them to glad to live. Just after they ultimately apprehend what's taking region, I lose them." – Gen X Female

The statements above show off that all of us input the frame of employees with our life stories and precise points of view. However, it's similarly clean that solutions to frustrations inside the workplace must encompass sitting all of the manner right down to ask pointed questions about now not simply priorities, but how those priorities can be achieved. What is vital and why is it essential? And each elements want to take part further with the motive of proper discovery and willpower to letting exchange occur.

Practical Suggestions for Millennial/Gen Y Employees

Not every person has a discern, supervisor, supporter, or mentor to assist manual and shape their career. Most mother and father are left to determine it out alongside the manner. As , no place of business will ever be satisfactory. However, a place of work can function correctly as long as expectations are aligned. And, at the same time as absolutely everyone has a chance to specific critiques and be heard, and paintings inside the route of answers and compromise. My examine indicates that most humans have excessive expectations in their managers and of the organisation or business enterprise wherein they artwork. It's virtually that the photograph of achievement can be special from character to man or woman.

Sometimes you need to compromise. You might also additionally want to sincerely get hold of conditions as they may be and broaden a plan to be triumphant with the equipment to be had to you. Compromise does now not want to indicate losing; perhaps you can find out center ground. Also, change may additionally take time. If you phrase ahead improvement, don't surrender.

Be accountable. Be high-quality you're doing what you're requested to do absolutely and in addition to you can. Requests for trade received't be received in case you're no longer doing all of your component within the eyes of your boss. If you need training, you could need to ask in undeniable language. If you could, volunteer for extra demanding situations to demonstrate your dedication to the agency and your non-public achievement.

Learn to navigate office politics. Office politics. You can't break out it or ignore it. But you can collect skills to better manage it. By now, you may have skilled or heard about activities wherein the less gifted, however maximum preferred person prevails or a seemingly unfair state of affairs takes area. Understand and be considerate approximately constructing your very private informal and formal networks. This isn't about recognition, but you may want to have get right of get right of entry to to to to people with data or have an effect on who allow you to. Invest in procedures to increase your emotional quotient or "EQ" (moreover referred to as emotional intelligence) so you are equipped with tool to observe and navigate the unwritten social cues that exist in each enterprise company, and can manage your response and reputation because of this.

Be cautious and smooth approximately what you ask for. Managers are problem-solvers. If you carry a problem with the answer you are trying to find, you may get what you want. But if you aren't clean, the solution might not be what you expect. Also, if you don't do your homework and present some issue that is simply outdoor of what the organization has finished before, your request can also need to end up useless on arrival.

Finding Success at the Job

Practical Suggestions for Supervisors of Gen Y/Millennials

Although the problems that get up can also seem trivial to you, your Millennial worker is stressed out to carry out his or her best art work at the identical time as sure situations are met. Facilitating an accommodating workplace may be your nice productivity booster and retention tool.

Create an first rate paintings setting. The paintings environment subjects to Millennials. Whether it's far the tone you placed or the culture at your office, this period isn't comfortable with a cold or sterile setting with a "punch the clock" and "heads down" fashion. They will be predisposed to appearance art work as an extension in their lives. Flexibility in approach, area, hours, and environment all make a difference in productiveness, tenure, and loyalty.

Be beneficiant with optimistic feedback. Remind your self that your Gen Y employee is used to all types of input with which to assess and make choices, and the maximum purchaser-splendid assets will win out. Make expert remarks, organization information, and appropriate training comfortably available. Plan methods to build up their mind and hire their choices to make the place of business and work technique as appealing and extremely good as possible.

Provide training. For many Millennials, the course to a brilliant function became a adventure. Now that they've arrived, they want to do properly. Training is an funding for your personnel and devices them up for success. The education can be achieved through you, via publications that your organization gives or outdoor assets. Don't count on them to ask for training; hold in mind making the funding in process capabilities and professional improvement to set them up for achievement.

Chapter 5: Attitudes About Other Generations At Work

Recently, there was greater hobby placed on generation-associated variations. When these variations are comprehended, bias may be identified and removed, and it's miles an lousy lot less complex to look what's required for the success of the project, the individual, the group, and the business agency. Human assets experts and leaders who really want to bring out the satisfactory in all their employees invest time in searching on the exquisite capabilities that each employee brings to their personnel. They make the effort to understand the type of needs, needs, and desires that need to be incorporated into their corporation to look achievement for the bottom line and for human beings. Overlooked disparities or opportunities can bring about war, even as popularity of variations is step one inside the route of powerful collaboration. Employers and personnel every must make aware efforts to recognize every distinctive's perspectives.

Of course, genuinely all people could have trouble seeing the terrible tendencies, or stereotypes, related to their personal era. One have to resultseasily recall that it's harder for one era to view every different with extra first-rate regard than horrible. Even so, my research decided some of quite generous intergenerational assessments.

They Said... We Said...

I invited the examine individuals to percentage their evaluations approximately their coworkers in each generational enterprise and asked Considering the multigenerational place of job, what's the BEST trouble about every generational group? In distinct terms, I gave every era the hazard to say some thing great approximately each different generation to benefit insights at the powerful attributes of each era organization.

When the responses came in, it turn out to be glaring how tough it is to allow move of first-rate bad biases. The responses, in area of strictly figuring out awesome subjects, have been a aggregate of pleasant, horrible, and impartial observations.

How Baby Boomers, Gen X, and Gen Z See Gen Y

In supplying their evaluations approximately Gen Y, the Baby Boomers, Gen X, and the Gen Z-ers stated all the common negative critiques about Millennials. However, there had been many astute observations made with the aid of the use of way of people of every era figuring out the high quality and precise strengths Gen Y brings to the table.

The majority of feedback focused on the Millennials' technical savvy and recognition, noting a pleasant. Their capability and willingness to consist of and adopt era—and a awful: stuck up in generation. An series of expressions via the use of every technology captured Millennial creativity and propensity for brand new mind.

Many respondents moreover mentioned that Millennials are inquisitive about training, in search of to study the whole lot they will, and that they may be enormously knowledgeable. A couple additionally stated that they've placed a focus on development and planning for retirement as amazing figuring out dispositions for Gen Y. The three generations also cited that Millennials have a tendency to be greater socially orientated, and that they're hardworking. On a lighter be conscious, at least one respondent in every generation, together with Gen Y, claimed that this period had the first rate track.

Baby Boomer Perspective on Gen Y: While the tech-savviness, balance, and effect had been stated, the Baby Boomers listed greater of the bad trends: lazy, assume everything need to be handed to them, leap from commercial enterprise agency to business enterprise, need what they need, don't care approximately walking, disrespectful and unappreciative, spoiled liberal brats.

Baby Boomer Insights

Technology ancient beyond

Wanting to make things higher and much less complicated

Blending younger ideas with maturity

Are nicely enough personnel, will be inclined to be task jumpers

Not afraid to ask questions or to call for authenticity

Teaches everybody else how the brand new tech can help us all

Balance

Gen X Perspective on Gen Y: Gen X diagnosed more emotional individual inclinations, which include excessive-strung, unhappy, frank, shy, honest, braveness, free-energetic, driven, and humble. Gen X moreover had some preference phrases: lazy oversensitive crybaby techno zombies, appearing like they are aware of it all. A quantity of Gen X respondents additionally said mainly that they relate to Gen Y in age.

Gen X Insights

Take care of the surroundings

New in place of work and potential to head an extended way

Innovative and positive

Empathetic to humans with youngsters

Gen Z Perspective on Gen Y: Gen Z said contradictions with their greater senior Gen Y opposite numbers. Gen Z had little or no awful to say approximately Gen Y. Gen Z diagnosed with Gen Y in phrases of sparkling mind and enthusiasm for modern day subjects. Some Gen Z perceived that Millennials grew up with each technology and minimum technology, had older and greater latest critiques, have each new and vintage traditions, modern/antique faculty style. It seems that to Gen Z, Millennials are visible as elders.

Gen Z Insights

Change makers

Give appropriate advice however also are relatable

This greater moderen technology can but train Gen Z

They started & maintain a wonderful deal of the social justice campaigns we understand these days.

How Gen Y Sees Themselves

Reflecting upon how individuals of Gen Y view the high-quality tendencies related to themselves, the Millennial respondents had an array of answers that meditated what the opportunity three generations had to mention approximately Gen Y. They go through in thoughts themselves to be:

Creative

Technologically savvy

Culturally orientated

Fighting for a better future

Shaping the world

Highly charge education

Eager

Hardworking

Socially oriented

A few other comments furnished more attributes and insights into the Millennial mind-set regarding their careers and contributions to the place of business:

Multidimensional

Striving to grow to be leaders

Changing perceptions of labor

Not afraid to do subjects out of doors the sector and take dangers

Cusp of making sufficient

Right in their excessive

More cultural businesses

Most of the remarks were forward searching and first-rate. However, there has been one stark reminder that many on this technology are having hassle locating jobs and wages commensurate with their education. They communicated it as a stop end result:

having a difficult life.

Taken collectively, the remarks tell us that Gen Y considers themselves to be motive-orientated, open to range, confident, and formidable explorers who are cause on changing what doesn't paintings within the worldwide at the equal time as securing their non-public futures.

How Gen Y Sees the Other Generation Groups

I moreover tested how Gen Y perspectives their extra senior and further younger coworkers. For the most element, Gen Y described each technology in complimentary terms.

Millennial attitude on Baby Boomers: With little or no negative to mention, the Millennials summed up the fast-to-be-retired Baby Boomers with many repetitions of the following expressions:

Hard jogging

Wise

Better values

Seasoned

Ethics

Life tales

Dedicated

Retiring quickly

Responsible

Traditional

Enjoyed life more

Money-clever

Expanded the economy

Perhaps the maximum complimentary homage provided to the Boomers modified into from a Gen Y Female: Can normally study subjects from them if you want to normally paintings till the surrender of time in the place of job and in actual lifestyles.

Millennial mind-set on Gen X: For the most element, Gen Y stated their right away elders, Gen X, with the equal form of recognize that they used describing the

Baby Boomers, offering variations of the following problems:

They are pass-getters

Hard human beings

Have remarkable enjoy

Knowledgeable

Good paintings ethic

Nice and satisfactory

Excellent leaders

Good humor

Role fashions

Willing to assist

Been there some time

Interestingly, Millennials decided Gen X to be extra "mature" (i.E., antique) than they decided the Boomers.

Stuck in antique strategies

Oldie song

They're too conservative

Do topics antique school

Although some decided Gen X to be contemporary and unfastened thinkers. At the equal time, Millennials noted a few Gen X obligation for the begin of change in place of work functioning and attitudes, along with the ones about paintings/existence balance, and range.

Beginning of era

The manner matters modified from prolonged in the beyond

Understand there's greater to existence than work

They offer specific ethnic companies and give you extra religious traditions.

Millennial mind-set on Gen Z: Gen Y mentioned Gen Z's youngsters, once in a while with records, occasionally with disparaging terms, calling them out for laziness, immaturity, and cluelessness. However, greater favored the Gen Z eagerness to study and paintings and their adaptable, teachable spirit with hundreds of functionality.

Most comments mentioned exquisite technical capacity, a few even acknowledging that Gen Z's competence outstripped their very personal.

Always a step ahead of the era company and commonly seeking out techniques to comprise the era in duties and duties.

This generation may be very clever and are more proficient than ever in advance than.

Think out of doors the field, more up to date on technology

New Century with new Technology and additional accomplishments

One Gen Y player entered the subsequent in each of the 3 areas provided for remarks approximately what they noticed as most extraordinary approximately each technology: I don't like organizations. This actually displays the Millennial aversion to labels, logos, or precise such variations.

In these verbatim replies, Gen Y shows themselves to be quite degree-headed and purpose in addition to observant. They don't begrudge acknowledging someone having better talents or excellent perspectives and supply credit score rating for tough art work and experience.

Implications for Work Success and Career Paths

The place of business is converting and being driven thru many elements, together with shifts in generational values. I studies the commonalities associated with the historical factors that help shape the values and possibilities of the awesome generations to facilitate data, ordinary performance, cooperation and profession achievement in the place of business. Workplaces which may be staffed through manner of all of the generations can find out masses of perspectives. An appreciation of various factors of view will enable coworkers to count on and observe awesome eventualities and put together for the destiny on the identical time as staying grounded and sensible.

Consider the following statements:

"The senior leader in a single employer scares me. I can't just pass as loads as her and ask her what she thinks about some of my thoughts. She is simply too essential all the time and the unstated rule is that you best communicate along with your boss and those at your diploma." – Gen Y Male

"I have become considering how we may need to get a number of us to paintings some distance flung hours with out shorting staff on the phones if clients need us. I'd supply it up, however I guess you the following day's paycheck that 1/2 of of oldsters will discover it impossible to resist and half of of folks will hate it, and also you apprehend who's going to be on which element." – Gen Y Female

"Why acquired't my more youthful employees open up approximately the mind I understand they have got that might make matters greater efficient spherical proper here? I run a decent deliver and overall performance is the choice of the game, however none of them ever approach me or maybe write some element within the place on their ordinary standard performance evaluations wherein I provide to allow them to proportion." – Gen X Female

"Our new manager simply stormed out the door due to the reality she didn't get her manner. In reality, she had a high-quality idea, however the delivery grow to be poorly achieved. We all hate place of work politics. But studying a manner to navigate it is crucial. You have to gather a network, realise a manner to compromise and save you taking the whole thing so for my part. It's not commonly about you; we absolutely don't have the finances right now. Millennials!" – Baby Boomer Male

In our age-diverse staff, traditional strategies of having paintings completed may be interpreted as "vintage college," as "traditional," or "smart" and new thoughts can be strong as "modern," "native," or "charge-brought" depending to your point of view. Intentional exploration of the perspectives of various generations need to be encouraged in region of disregarded with out considerate interest.

Building a Support Network

Think ofpeople internal your agency who you understand and could help you discover and plan your career trajectory. One of these humans can be your boss; a few other may be some different worker who's been with the corporation for a long term.

Arrange to have a conversation with them in the route of a time that does not intrude together together with your (or their) artwork duties. Tell them you'd need to proportion what you admire about them and what they do, and ask them inside the event that they might be open to helping you to analyze more.

Remember to comply with up and to thank them for his or her assist. If they refuse your request, even though be polite and discover someone else to invite.

Practical Suggestions for Supervisors of Gen Y/Millennials

While many or maximum strategies are nicely mounted, innovation in spite of the reality that performs a major role in gaining a competitive benefit. Make an attempt to be open to contributions from Gen Y employees that stem from their everyday contributions, and their functionality to method subjects in new tactics. Millennials are settling into their careers, but are although open to studying.

Share high quality comments. Lead Gen Y in continuing to broaden a robust existence-lengthy paintings ethic through placing clear expectations and imparting incentives and examples. Specific feedback and in reality suitable correction are beneficial, after you make an effort to pay interest and recognize in which your younger human beings are coming from.

Respect guidelines the day. Gen Y is aware of respectful, as-equals interplay, no longer inflexible command-and-manage methods. They want to make contributions meaningfully and be diagnosed for the fee they upload, but if they're demeaned or unheard, they may be less willing to reply well to what you're saying.

Accept that the place of work is an extension in their lives. It is greater than only a challenge. Expect to must deal with subjects apart from the paintings approach. More and greater employees find administrative center way of life to be as critical, if not greater crucial, than the paintings they do and the compensation they get keep of. Even if this seems beside the factor to you, don't forget that your Gen Y employees will look elsewhere if an excessive amount of is unattractive about their entire paintings enjoy.

Questions for Supervisors of Millennials/Gen Y to Consider

Chapter 6: Career Advice/Reflection

Born from 1981 to 1995, Millennials are certainly approximately 21 to 36 years antique, simply coming out of college to about 10 years into their walking profession. All of them have probably been across the block enough to have heard a fantastic deal of career recommendation and positioned a number of it into practice. With dreams and dreams indoors acquire, they may be growing in their career, identifying their splendid practices, skills, and options and getting to know important career and life instructions. They realise what form of information resonates with them and the form of control they recognize and need to emulate.

It has been stated that revel in is the notable instructor. If we heed the instructions that can be taught from achievement and failure, we will prepare for future fulfillment. To assemble on the collective reviews of the Millennials in this look at, I asked the individuals of Gen Y What is the pleasant career recommendation that you have received?

Learning from Others: Best Advice Gen Y Has Received

The most repeated sentiment become to never give up, which became taken into consideration the amazing recommendation through manner of 12% of the respondents. The subsequent maximum repeated nugget of advice have grow to be to find and do what you love, with 10% of the Millennial people locating this maximum treasured. Eight percent of the respondents observed the first-class advice in admonitions to place inside the most attempt to get the tremendous very last outcomes, including normally supply a hundred percent and in case you fall, get proper decrease lower back up, and to constantly deal with your method as even though it turned into your very private commercial enterprise and in no way preserve lower back.

About 15% of the Millennials favored recommendation centered on coping with private limitations and private expectancies. There were strongly worded encouragements to:

Focus on yourself, your personal commercial enterprise commercial enterprise corporation, and now not others, i.E., overlook about chatter/advice from folks that don't understand my path.

Expect errors, study from them and circulate on, i.E., constantly take delivery of high high-quality complaint and do not forget you may in no manner be satisfactory and will usually want to decorate an trouble of your self.

Be flexible and inclined to alternate your career or plan, i.E., be adaptable and inclined to change or draw near new possibilities.

Ignore the naysayers, i.E., don't allow human beings's ignorant perceptions of you to save you you from making it to the top.

A few of the opposite jewels of information furnished embody:

Become a powerful philosopher

Put yourself within the different man's shoes

Live like I am death!

To paintings greater hard until your idols become your opposition

Own it

Work in silence, permit your noise be your fulfillment

Make connections and don't be afraid to invite your connections questions

This is genuinely your first step

If you're 5 min. Early you are late. My mentor typically stated in case you wait spherical for everybody else to step up before you step up you may usually lose your spot

To do the very notable I can, and launch myself from in search of to manage each little detail

Lessons Gen Y Has Learned, So Far...

Self-reflected photo can be an essential element of career development. It lets in the opportunity to recognize what is important and what are the limitations or distractions, and wherein one desires to transport subsequent. It exposes the crucial factor elements wished to devise a route forward. To get a mindset on which kinds of advice people of Gen Y positioned beneficial, I asked them to provide recommendation for his or her greater younger selves. I asked If you can bypass again in time, what advice should you supply yourself on the begin of your career?

It is plain that Millennials are aware of the effect of training, cash, and profession choices on their lives. The magnificence of excellent recommendation that became most usually noted needed to do with university, with 24 instances (15%). The responses were every modern-day day and unique:

Go to high school for the right hassle

Stay in university

Go back to highschool NOW!

Improve your check dependancy

Start in advance in getting college out of the way

Four humans named precise degrees that they might have suggested themselves to pursue from the start. This is a warning to be extra aware about the necessities to your career early on.

The next maximum common reply (8%) became a plea to begin college earlier or get into their profession earlier, and try to support quicker. Eleven (7%) respondents mentioned money in their replies, 8 of which had been about saving greater and earlier. Three gave themselves interest searching tips, andreferred to as on themselves to expect extra absolutely approximately what they in truth desired and to make a better career choice.

Start faster

Get into this profession in advance, and enjoy greater manner alternatives early on

Start looking for a better characteristic faster

Give myself a strong plan for saving coins

To assume greater approximately my strengths and what I actually favored to gain earlier than embarking on a profession course

Between three and eight percentage of check individuals would possibly have informed themselves to

Work difficult (eight%)

Be open minded and no longer to accept an awful lot much less because of doubts that there is some component else or due to worry (7%)

Learn extra on the activity (five%)

Don't give up (five%)

Be extra verbally assertive (5%)

Do some thing you want (four%)

Be yourself (three%)

Five percent must have given themselves recommendation approximately getting along aspect others. Only four members, three%, had terms approximately finding paintings/existence stability.

"I hopped round jobs proper out of university. Part of that became worrying conditions confronted finding any method, however I'd push myself to apply for greater. I in all likelihood applied for 20 or so jobs out of university and idea that grow to be tough. After hating my first two jobs, I applied for over 70 jobs in a month to discover a hollow at my contemporary employer enterprise, which aligns with my career goals. I had this feel of entitlement that I'd truely get a exquisite procedure when I graduated...and it's now not that smooth." – Gen Y Female

This final indexed reaction embodies a bargain of what Millennials confronted of their first few jobs and face now in getting traction of their careers. However, the most not unusual replies indexed above make it smooth that Millennials are aware of what it takes. Admonitions to artwork difficult, be open-minded, and not settle moreover remind us that this era is nicely equipped to deal with their state of affairs and acquire what they need.

Implications for Work Success and Career Paths

Gen Y's eyes are giant open in terms of facts how hard some of their cohort have struggled with negative venture markets, college debt, and the general and lasting consequences of undergo markets, but they will be even though determined to chase their dreams and find fulfillment on their very own terms. They understand their success is as a lot as their non-public tough paintings, and at the same time, they are committed to involvement with corporations they may recognize and get in the back of.

Look once more on the numbers of those above who maximum valued such admonitions to art work difficult, be open minded, look at more, now not surrender, and so forth. This is 34% of Millennials who locate reminders of some type of personal strength of thoughts to be maximum useful in looking ahead. Probably the easiest issue supervisors and managers of Millennials can do is to truly and frequently encourage them to hold striving and no longer settle, to bear in mind in themselves, and to move for what they want. Everyone goals encouragement, even folks who are doing properly.

Part of this encouragement is achievement together with to achievement. Both employees and their bosses can artwork together to discover possibilities that permit Gen Y to accumulate accomplishments and additions to their information sets. These achievements upload no longer nice to character resumes, however additionally to normal enterprise improvement.

Education figures strongly within the Gen Y psyche. It is called vitally essential, even whilst the efforts for some have now not led to higher pay or perhaps paintings inside the desired trouble. Both Millennials and their supervisors can find out techniques to help advancing schooling. First, there may be methods to understand formal training attained in different fields via seeking out tactics to combine that with modern-day paintings. Secondly, for folks that remorse deeply that they will be no longer going for walks within the subject they studied for, it isn't too late to trying to find a trade. And for folks that do now not have the formal education or who need to have a look at extra, supervisors could make efforts to provide cross-training possibilities or offer employer assist (repayment of schooling or expenses, and flex-time) for out of doors instructions that complement and improve modern-day competencies.

Creating a Career Reassessment Map

As you construct your profession, it's frequently useful to step lower back and check whether or now not you're wherein you idea you'd be. Complete the chart underneath and then ask for enter from a person you do not forget.

Practical Suggestions for Millennial/Gen Y Employees

Above all, take into account that your Gen Y people are nonetheless new of their careers. You can function a powerful position version, mentor, educate, and sponsor.

Be to be had for your Gen Y employees. Let your personnel realize which you are interested in them and inspire them to ask questions. Make positive you have time set apart to be available for your institution and tell them of your availability. When you meet with them, be prepared to collect their criticisms and pointers as masses as you'd like them to acquire yours, and be organized to be obvious approximately enterprise enterprise rules and recognition.

Build Gen Y's self-efficacy. Self-efficacy relates to someone's belief of their capability to perform nicely and play a extremely good characteristic in how one techniques their system and problem-solves. Find out what's important on your Gen Y worker and renowned their contributions. Find methods to behave as a sounding board at the identical time as they are attempting to observe and make options. Offer possibilities to even the most tentative man or woman to try new matters and take dangers with out fear of failure. Repeated reviews with fulfillment will assemble their self assurance and overall performance over time.

Challenge them. Point out regions wherein this or that motion can function them for development up or laterally, and encourage them to stretch themselves. Support tactics your worker can boom their records thru education, direction paintings, or stretch

assignments.

Chapter 7: Everyone Has Something To Offer

As we look at the multigenerational place of business, it's important to recognize what can sell intergenerativity at work (i.E., sharing exchange throughout limitations that normally separate discourse, and tapping the strength that could give up end result from connecting in any other case divergent fields of human business enterprise).Fifty nine The key is for each Gen Y personnel and their supervisors and coworkers to bear in thoughts that there may be normally multiple mindset to be considered, every as legitimate as the following. A efficient and exquisite growth revel in needn't be considered an impossibility.

Everyone involved can renowned their private views, but moreover deliberately set them apart in the hobby of records others. Clear conversation about desires and expectancies can contribute to the establishment of commonplace dreams and the method of engaging in them. The purpose to recognize and cooperate is vital, and refusal to step out of doors one's comfort quarter or to compromise will nullify progress. This is real inside the realm of personal improvement or that of group or organizational fulfillment.

Members of Gen Y are captivated with being involved and creating a distinction in procedures which can be important to them. Many want to determine to a single organisation for some of years, so it is probably well well sincerely really worth the investment of schooling and mentoring Millennial personnel. While a few Millennials are but younger and green in some processes, they've their regions of statistics to hold to the administrative center. Others were spherical lengthy sufficient to have a robust draw near in their particular place of job manner of life and potential gadgets, and are ready to cope with leadership roles. Their comfort with and information of technology in addition to familiarity with the "vintage college" should make administrative center increase smoother than for those working from best one attitude.

Key Takeaways

Happiness, relationships, doing nicely of their function, repayment, and method delight are most essential for Gen Y, and due to this, a sturdy paintings/existence balance will parent cautiously into personal and profession selections. Inclusion and justice are alsolenses thru which Gen Y examine interest options. Millennials consider themselves a part of a larger gadget inner which they need to discover a manner to live and contribute meaningfully. In this way, high-quality best themselves isn't a given.

Gen Y believes that the American Dream is rather handy to them, however they understand truly that a good way to acquire it, they may must paintings difficult to seize up or alter their view of the American Dream a piece.

As with personnel of any age, Gen Y personnel want a manager who will respect and resource them with kindness, accurate management, and flexibility. Adequate education and a platform for constructing achievement, coupled with superb and optimistic criticism, are crucial. Mentorship geared toward getting them ready to cope with greater duty and input manage roles is also key in assisting this period Millennial be successful.

A few cautioned every day reminders for Gen Y personnel in the place of job:

You are converting the administrative center, and it makes many people concerned. It is your opportunity. Remember that maximum anyone, alongside aspect your boss, can be viewing you and interacting with you from biases and expectations he or she could likely location upon others, for some factor motive. This won't be sincere, however many research display that it exists. In spite of the stereotypes, your era has already made changes which might be lasting as customers and as employees. Be aware of this possibility for your interactions with others, and maintain the ones biases from impeding the achievement you're after.

You can construct the career you want. You realise through way of the use of now what it will take to reap your dreams, and there can be no time similar to the existing to show yourself in that you're now or to are looking for a characteristic better appropriate on your everyday desires.

Careers are journeys and setbacks can provide precious boom and instructions for you. In many times, your first few jobs may not be profession material. However, there may be a few factor to be determined at every system, so do your best at every stop. If you've made mistakes, the first-rate reaction is to examine and expand from them. With your hard work ethic and willingness to take probabilities at the same time as possibilities come alongside, you'll be pretty licensed to step into your best feature whilst it gives itself.

Position your self for the position and profession you need. Continue to pursue the expertise and schooling you want so that you may be successful for your function, and locate ways to make a contribution to the achievement of the organization. If you still do your remarkable and also you received't have regrets that could impact your achievement later. If you have got intentions to live collectively together along with your business enterprise, it is going to be critical to have a plan for quick-time period and prolonged-term fulfillment. In most instances, it's miles going to be as much as you to make that plan. Seek assist from experienced coworkers, your human resources department, or a mentor.

It is OK if you don't realise what you need to be at the same time as you increase up. The superb recommendation I received in my overdue twenties come to be to be open to possibilities. Make sure your plan and your network permit for possibilities to go back your manner that can take you places you couldn't have even dreamed of however. Be high-quality to study your profession plan periodically so you can diploma your improvement. Stay in touch with experts and others whose critiques you charge who can guide you and help you view your questions and issues via tremendous lenses. Whatever you do, don't give up.

Suggested Actions for Gen Y to Take

Remember your priorities. You charge every the compensation in your artwork and the time invested with own family and buddies. Unfortunately, it is going to suggest that you ought to make change-offs and be thoughtful in the way you manipulate your lifestyles in order that one choice doesn't come on the charge of the alternative. Take a touch time to undergo in thoughts what is critical to you and learn how to return to terms with alternate-offs that you locate best.

Invest to your destiny. Baby Boomers are leaving the staff and Gen X on my own can't address the void that stays. Invest in training and schooling and pursue visible achievement absolutely so you'll be first in line as your business employer seems to your technology to step up.

Build and hold your help device. Ask the a achievement people you respect in the occasion that they'd mentors or function fashions arising over time. Chances are nicely that their answer may be an unqualified "Yes." Your assist gadget should encompass those like-minded friends and family individuals you could vent to, however additionally enterprise professionals and different quite a success folks that will project you and can help you know the truth, in place of genuinely allow you to understand topics are awesome. Some of your network will come and pass, and a few can be with you all the time. It might be important that you stay connected and proactively manipulate the relationships.

Have a contingency plan. As you recognize from experience in down markets and with intervals of challenge shortage, nothing is confident, even at the same time as you do the whole lot right. Do your extremely good to set up strong plans to maintain cash for your future. If vital, trim down your contemporary-day way of life for you to do so. So assume to have 3 to 6 months of your dwelling prices in monetary economic financial savings.

A Few Suggested Daily Reminders for Supervisors of Gen Y inside the Workplace:

Remember that your Gen Y employee is simply now solidly settled into his or her profession, clever in some techniques and however green in others. Most of your employees will fast be Millennial and Gen Z. Remember that those more youthful personnel will wield quite a few affect inside the coming a long time. Viewing them as valued group members will make it less complex to welcome their contributions.

The place of business has superior. It's no longer constantly incorrect, it's simply awesome. Keep an open thoughts. Try to view Millennial mind you will be uncomfortable with as in reality that—particular—and not as terrible or willful battle of phrases. Find common ground for difficult conversations and allow them to teach you some thing new.

Be a train and version extremely good control practices. Encourage and version best strategies on what it takes to be successful. Offer positive grievance and guidelines for achievement. Gen Y is calling and that they strongly expect that you'll be a md they could look up to and appreciate.

Expect appropriate subjects to seem. Be affected individual. Being open to new thoughts can propel your branch to extra productiveness or maybe towards a actual leap forward. It also can take more communication and a fake start or , however perseverance can pay off in the end.

Practical Suggestions for Supervisors of Millennials/Gen Y

Adjust your expectancies. Millennials are involved about doing well of their roles and receiving appropriate feedback and repayment, so keep to relate to them in this degree. However, they will be moreover concerned with the larger photograph, which incorporates cultural troubles as they effect the place of business, racially charged conditions, moral company behavior, and social connection, as an instance. Technology might also even determine into the adjustments Millennials need to appearance take place. If you could pass proactively in your industrial employer company to recognize and encompass the ones realities, capacity upheaval due to misaligned employee expectations may be minimized and excessive high-quality consequences determined out faster.

Communicate greater. Discussions approximately each day commercial agency issues will in no manner depart, but Millennials will determine on extra transparency at the desk than you may be aware about sharing. They will request feedback as to their artwork performance, but additionally they want very clean steerage as to what it takes to get earlier and how development is compensated. They need to see that their work is really tied to anticipated results, and could likely ask questions that could seem unrelated to you, however that have import for them.

Build real relationships. Relationship depend. Millennials are more likely to view you, their supervisor, as an same, and as a teach and be an awful lot less involved approximately protocols and greater cushty with sharing opinion. Work is a set attempt, not a pinnacle down type method. Your Gen Y employee can also be interested in your personal life, because paintings/life balance is vital to them and it includes own family and free-time hobbies.

Finally

Gen Y in all fairness informed, properly grounded, and already privy to the effect that they'll be making on the labor strain over the following couple of some years. In spite of a hard start for lots, maximum people of Gen Y are excellent in phrases of their personal success and attainment of their model of the American Dream. They have experienced and witnessed the effect of the financial bust on Baby Boomer and Gen X own family individuals, so they may be practical, sensible, and as it need to be cautious, however unwilling to lie down and give up.

The Millennial technology believes that first-rate accomplishments and trade are inevitable. They are ready with progressive generation, brief get admission to to facts approximately simply a few trouble they want to apprehend, and the severa views in their pals. With the guiding ideas of justice, tolerance, ethical conduct, and a important vicinity for family and buddies, the hallmark of this era is probably the transfiguration of the American administrative center as we're aware about it now.

While it'll take time for generally held terrible evaluations to subside, my studies did thousands to belie common attitudes that make more potent terrible perceptions about Millennials; instead, it positioned out a super Millennial sense of responsibility and self-course that, if harnessed properly, will certainly make the administrative center a better place for generations to come back.

Millennial/Gen Y Action Plan

1. Preparing for Success

2. Setting Priorities

In this situation, if all subjects have been identical, transferring to the modern-day activity seems like an smooth choice with a score of "11." However, even as factors together with excursion, benefits, and challenge come into play, the choice to stay on your cutting-edge function with a multiplier score of "28" may also additionally win out and lead you to interact in a bit more idea about what genuinely topics at this element.

3. Finding Success on the Job

4. Building a Support Network

Think ofpeople inner your organization who you understand and will help you discover and plan your profession trajectory. One of these humans can be your boss; every exceptional may be every other employee who's been with the company for a long time.

Arrange to have a verbal exchange with them during a time that doesn't intrude along with your (or their) paintings obligations. Tell them you'd want to percent what you understand approximately them and what they do, and ask them in the occasion that they might be open to helping you to have a look at extra.

Remember to comply with up and to thank them for his or her assist. If they do no longer want your request, nonetheless be well mannered and find out a person else to invite.

5. Creating a Career Reassessment Map

As you construct your career, it's regularly beneficial to step returned and determine whether or not you're in which you notion you'd be. Complete the chart under and then ask for enter from someone you believe.

Checklist for Supervisors

The place of work has advanced. It's not necessarily incorrect; it's simply particular. Try to view the Millennial mind you will be uncomfortable with as without a doubt that—tremendous—and not as terrible or willful conflict of words. Find common floor for difficult conversations and let them train you some thing new.

Be a train and version appropriate leadership practices. Encourage and version effective techniques on what it takes to gain fulfillment. Offer high-quality criticism and recommendations for success. Gen Y is looking and they strongly anticipate that you'll be a boss they might look up to and admire.

Expect accurate topics to expose up. Being open to new thoughts can propel your branch to greater productivity or perhaps to a actual soar in advance. It may additionally take more communication and a faux start or , but perseverance pays off ultimately.

Set them up for achievement. Perhaps even as you began out your career, the expectancies for personnel were one-of-a-type than they will be in recent times. You may want to probable have entered the place of job with an in-intensity training software or you might have been left to trouble-clear up on your non-public. Surviving an ordeal thru fireplace experience isn't usually a badge of honor for Millennials. If they may be irritated and might't see a route inside the route of sustained fulfillment, they'll depart.

Encourage the sensible components of career improvement and placed the plan in area. Due to the monetary device, many Millennials have had a delayed start to their careers and are honestly keen to capture up. Think of methods to reinforce proper artwork behavior and competencies that allows you to serve them properly in any challenge, not in reality in your department. Millennials have several years under their belt and feature expectancies about developing in their roles and careers.

Be obvious about reimbursement. Financial safety is essential to your Millennial worker, and so they may be centered on improvement and bonuses. It may be vital to have conversations approximately reimbursement in all office work (e.G., earnings, bonuses, excursion, different benefits) to govern their expectancies.

Recognize how they will be fashioned thru key non-public and expert values. From a personal attitude, happiness and relationships ranked pretty for Gen Y. Professionally, Gen Y values making extra cash and doing nicely in their modern-day function. As you keep in mind the crew environment and your control style, don't forget how the nice of your interactions and the paintings enjoy will rely quantity for your Millennial employees. Coaching them to excel on the hobby and being smooth approximately their possibilities to earn extra cash may be key to retention.

Offer constructive comments at the same time as it's miles warranted. Generation Y is used to instantaneous remarks for his or her mind because of their commonplace use of social media within the path in their youth. Give them what they want to without a doubt carry out what you're asking of them, together with encouraging terms. Be thoughtful approximately requests for better or particular art work, and make sure you furthermore may percentage honest assurances regarding what you recognize about their artwork.

Be clear about their options. Be positive to permit them to recognise they are valued of their contemporary function and be inclined to be open and realistic approximately their career possibilities. Whether you're offering assignment alternatives inside your organization or laterally inside your organization, inspire your personnel to find out and do what they're able to to location themselves for moving on in the event that they have got mastered their present day function. Coach them to transport sideways while you could, and be supportive in their picks to move on in the occasion that they do.

Support circle of relatives and work-life balance. Allow flexibility with paintings schedules. Relationships and happiness are extraordinarily critical to your Millennial workers, so be cautious to now not treat the ones as afterthoughts on your interactions along with your group individuals. Gen Y-ers who experience that you rate what they price can be extra satisfied and more likely to head the extra mile for you.

Create a platform for problem-solving. Make time to pay interest on your Millennials and get their ideas approximately what's taking place with the department and the business corporation. Answer their hard questions as top notch you may and address their court docket instances and troubles. Keep an open mind as you solicit their enter.

Create an first-rate artwork putting. The paintings environment topics to Millennials. Whether it is the tone you place or the way of life at your place of job, this technology isn't cushty with a cold or sterile setting with a "punch the clock" and "heads down" fashion. They have a propensity to look art work as an extension of their lives.

Flexibility in approach, vicinity, hours, and surroundings all make a distinction in productivity, tenure, and loyalty.

Be generous with exceptional feedback. Remind yourself that your Gen Y worker is used to all forms of enter with which to evaluate and make alternatives, and the most person-incredible assets will win out. Make expert remarks, employer statistics, and suitable education effortlessly to be had. Plan processes to build up their mind and make use of their alternatives to make the place of business and art work way as appealing and best as feasible.

Provide education. For many Millennials, the path to a truely exceptional characteristic grow to be a journey. Now that they've arrived, they want to do properly. Training is an funding on your personnel and gadgets them up for success. The schooling can be finished by means of the usage of you, thru courses that your corporation offers or outside sources. Don't watch for them to ask for education; keep in mind making the funding in project skills and expert improvement to set them up for achievement.

Capitalize on their strengths.

Are you the usage of each employee to their fullest? Try to set up duties and structures to utilize your Gen Y employee's talents to their fullest, along with annoying situations as properly. Solicit their ideas as to the manner to enhance techniques and cause them to chargeable for enforcing the exchange.

Be aware that every one your actions depend. Command and manage patterns don't seem to play nicely with Gen Y. Employees pay close to hobby to the manner you behavior your self. Your conduct and control will shape the future of your enterprise and the place of business. A respectful and supportive supervisor will bring out your Gen Y personnel' excellent efforts, and they could turn out to be your extremely good prolonged-term belongings.

Share incredible remarks. Lead Gen Y in continuing to extend a sturdy lifestyles-lengthy work ethic via placing easy expectancies and offering incentives and examples. Specific feedback and without a doubt apt correction are beneficial, after you take the time to pay attention and apprehend in which your greater younger human beings are coming from.

Respect rules the day. Gen Y is aware of respectful, as-equals interaction, now not inflexible command-and-manipulate techniques. They want to make a contribution meaningfully and be recognized for the value they add, but if they'll be demeaned or unheard, they'll be less willing to reply properly to what you're announcing.

Accept that the place of job is an extension of their lives. It is more than nice a gadget.

Expect to ought to cope with topics apart from the art work way. More and additional personnel discover administrative center way of life to be as vital, if now not extra vital, than the paintings they do and the reimbursement they reap. Even if this appears beside the point to you, preserve in thoughts that your Gen Y personnel will appearance a few special region if too much is unattractive approximately their whole art work enjoy.

Adjust your expectancies. Millennials are involved approximately doing well in their roles and receiving appropriate comments and repayment, so maintain to relate to them on this degree. However, they are moreover involved with the larger picture, which incorporates cultural problems as they effect the place of business, racially charged situations, moral enterprise behavior, and social connection, as an instance. Technology may even figure into the changes Millennials need to appearance get up. If you can circulate proactively on your enterprise employer to recognize and embody those realities, ability upheaval due to misaligned employee expectations can be minimized and high high-quality effects found out quicker.

Communicate more. Discussions about each day employer issues will in no manner depart, but Millennials will decide on greater transparency on the desk than you may be familiar with sharing. They will request feedback as to their art work ordinary average performance, but similarly they need very easy steerage as to what it takes to get beforehand and the way development is compensated. They need to see that their paintings is surely tied to predicted outcomes, and could probably ask questions that would appear unrelated to you, but that have import for them.

Chapter 8: Define "Generation"

While the idea of generations modified into referred to in ancient Egyptian and Greek texts, the contemporary test changed into inspired by using way of German sociologist Karl Mannheim in the 1950's.1 A "technology" is more than a fixed of people who percentage comparable years of beginning, it's miles the collective experience fashioned by using using historical and social contexts. Traditionalists have been normal via the World Wars whilst Millennials grew up during 911 and the begin of the internet. These formative reviews installation worldviews, values, and commonplace traits. However, there's a big range of perfect starting years that make up the Millennial era and there are conflicting evaluations about what makes them unique. Also, most studies has been finished in Western contexts and little is understood about Millennial values the world over.

Ignore the Stereotypes

In some techniques, Baby Boomers (born round 1946- 1964) and Generation Xers (born round 1965-1981) appear to be polar opposites of Millennials (born spherical 1982-2000). Yet, it isn't possible to generalize a set of one.Eight billion humans in the path of the globe3 or over eighty million United States citizens9. Studies on generational variations are inconsistent and plenty of pupils have pressured whether or not or no longer those stereotypes honestly exist inside the place of work.1 Other factors like socioeconomic beauty, gender, religion, persona and lifestyles level might also play huge roles in workplace dynamics than generational variations. There are a few key generational developments that can assist paint a sizable photograph of approaches a Millennial may also additionally behave in paintings situations, but it is critical to do not forget that all Millennials are not technological wizards similar to all Baby Boomers aren't workaholics.

Utilize the Technologically-Savvy

Communication and era flair and alertness is one of the most undisputed generational variations.1 As digital natives, the "Look at Me" technology maximum self-identifies with era use.Sixteen About half of of say they despatched or obtained a text message over the telephone in the beyond day, about double the share of Generation Xers.8 They are skilled with conversation technology, the internet, pc programs, cellular telephone applications and social media— and they realise it. This technological know-how can be useful as you dream up new techniques to higher achieve your task.

Harness their Creativity

You don't need to have arcades or sleeping pods to get progressive (even though, running at Google wouldn't be awful).Thirteen From concept-producing area journeys to Pixar's "non-public venture days" wherein personnel are given time to artwork on some thing they want to, there are plenty of strategies to encourage originality inside the place of work.2 Studies recommend, based totally totally on their age and particular testimonies, Millennials will be predisposed to illustrate greater outside-of-the-discipline wondering and are extra liable to undertaking norms that would reason a few high-quality breakthroughs to your place of job.1

Radiate Passion

If you're a chief, it's your duty and privilege to invite your organisation into your imaginative and prescient. Bill Hybels, author of Courageous Leadership and founder of the Global Leadership Summit, says "It's your mission to hold your ardour heat. Do a few element you need to do, study a few aspect you have to have a look at, pass anywhere you need to go to stay fired up."6 That form of passion is contagious. As a leader, you get to set the tone of your corporation. As Michael Jordan said, "Earn your management every day".

Anticipate the Commitment Issues

Disloyalty is simply one of the maximum important court docket cases about Generation Y. Baby Boomers fee difficult paintings and consistency while Millennials (and Generation Xers) thrive in environments of trade, profession mobility and flexibility. They are greater inspired by means of the use of a purpose than a particular commercial enterprise business enterprise and ninety one% will be predisposed to stay with a organisation for masses less than three years.Nine In reality, the not unusual Millennial will keep 7 remarkable jobs via age 26.Eleven

However, it's miles crucial no longer to good deal existence stage on the equal time as discussing organisation loyalty. In popular, loyalty toward employers has decreased over every technology.15 This is much more likely to reflect the reality that people generally will be inclined to decide at the familiar and are seeking out balance with improved age and duty. The idea of analyzing a present day alternate and socializing with a new organization of human beings is regularly less appealing at a later lifestyles diploma.15 Some studies argue that Millennials' loyalty is much like unique generations at comparable a while.15 Regardless of the reasons, it's far critical to observe that Millennials normally tend to update frequently among businesses. But there are procedures to combat this higher turnover goal. On pinnacle of imparting truthful repayment and difficult paintings, corporations that invest in career improvement, mentorship opportunities and stepped forward worker engagement are better able to preserve Millennials.1

Chapter 9: Accept the Facts

Before designing education packages or filling roles on your team, it can be useful to perceive some of information approximately Millennials. 34% of Millennials have as a minimum a bachelor's diploma which makes them the maximum knowledgeable generation to date.14 This diploma of schooling can make them appear overly-confident or possibly entitled. However, their unemployment rate is shape of double that of the us not unusual which may additionally moreover purpose a greater preference for solid positions.Eleven Most research agree that they price institution artwork, range, flexibility, training, and artwork-existence balance.15

Remember your Story

Reminiscing approximately your very very own beyond and opinions may additionally moreover help you empathize with Millennials. When you have got been 25, what were you struggling with or studying?

Who have been a few feature models in your life and how did they encourage and encourage you? Also be sensitive to the reality that these younger human beings aren't you. They have precise backgrounds, fears and passions, so don't assignment your very personal reviews onto them. You can also have walked up a hill, within the snow, every strategies when you had been a toddler, but recognize that each era has its non-public struggles on top of the ordinary age-related demanding situations.

Provide Flexibility

Millennials price flexibility in paintings hours, verbal exchange and kinds of responsibilities. Working remotely is turning into more commonplace sooner or later of every generation and a majority of Millennials need so that you can set their very very own paintings hours.Nine They additionally stability artwork and existence extra fluidly than Baby Boomers who determine upon a easy branch amongst non-public and professional.1 The use of technological gear has impacted conversation and advanced the capability to multitask life and artwork responsibilities simultaneously. Some studies endorse that the trend in the direction of greater accommodating paintings schedules is intergenerational.1 Allowing flexibility is appealing to capability personnel of all ages and may result in higher assignment delight. As prolonged because the procedure is getting completed properly, a extra comfortable artwork time table might be properly worth considering.

"Millennials aspire to marry the blue skies thinking about the Boomers with the grass-roots mind-set of GenX."

Mal Fletcher

Gain Perspective

Every man or woman operates from a selected worldview and people disparities appear more large even as progressed across generational lines. Millennials had been criticized for not sharing the same critiques about time, organisation organisation allegiance or artwork ethic as their older colleagues. However, they absolutely view and outline place of business fulfillment in every different way. Learning to inspire and relate to the Millennials for your place of business also can assist offer prolonged-term sustainability.

Educate Them

For masses of reasons, "actual life" appears particular to Millennials than to older generations when they have been similar a while. 1 out of 10 Millennials will buy a home earlier than age 30.Eleven 1 in five are married and most effective 12% have youngsters.11 They have turn out to be married and beginning households later than their predecessors.7 This can be a mirrored photograph on soaring divorce expenses or the growing commonplace quantity of student debt which make marriage and parenthood appear unappealing or not feasible. There is also a greater reputation, in particular for girls, on growing careers greater more youthful. Regardless, Millennials ought to use guidance from their elders in navigating the actual worldwide as they mature as employees, spouses, parents and adults in great.

Know the Financial Concerns

In 2011, more than 50% of Millennials had over \$35,000 in pupil loan debt.Sixteen Most of Generation Y believes that they may in no way see a pension or get hold of cash from Social Security.1 In slight of this great financial burden, greater younger employees are craving each hobby safety and financial knowledge. You must entice Millennials via way of manner of presenting 401k programs, providing monetary seminars and developing partnerships with universities to lower diploma fees. Also make certain that the desired diploma indexed within the challenge description shows the location's pay scale, an internship or assistant function need to not necessitate a draw close's degree.

Explore New Opportunities

Millennials art work properly on teams— take gain of their willingness to leap in! Have you been considering growing a summer time spirit week to decorate agency morale or beginning a volleyball group to construct network? Look to the Millennials to provide mind and exuberance for those initiatives.